TEACHERS' WORK

By the same author

Which Way Is Up? Essays on sex, class and culture (1983)
Making the Difference: Schools, families and social division (1982), with D.J. Ashenden, S. Kessler and G.W. Dowsett
Ockers and Disco-Maniacs: Sex, gender and secondary schooling (1982), with S. Kessler, D.J. Ashenden and G.W. Dowsett
Class Structure in Australian History (1980), with T.H. Irving
Socialism and Labor (1978)
Ruling Class, Ruling Culture: Studies of conflict, power and hegemony in Australian life (1977)
Twelve to Twenty: A study of teenagers in Sydney (1975), with W.F. Connell, R.E. Stroobant, K.E. Sinclair and K.W. Rogers
The Child's Construction of Politics (1971)
Politics of the Extreme Right: Warringah 1966 (1967), with F. Gould

Teachers' Work

R.W.CONNELL

Based on research done jointly with
D.J. Ashenden, S. Kessler and G.W. Dowsett

GEORGE ALLEN & UNWIN
SYDNEY LONDON BOSTON

First published in 1985
George Allen & Unwin Australia Pty Ltd
8 Napier Street, North Sydney, NSW 2060, Australia

George Allen & Unwin (Publishers) Ltd
Park Lane, Hemel Hempstead, Herts HP2 4TE, England

Allen & Unwin Inc.
Fifty Cross Street, Winchester, Mass 01890, USA

National Library of Australia
Cataloguing-in-Publication entry:

Connell, R.W. (Robert William), 1944–   .
  Teachers' work.

  Bibliography.
  Includes index.
  ISBN 0 86861 752 0.
  ISBN 0 86861 760 1 (pbk).

  1. High school teaching — Australia. 2. Educational
  sociology — Australia. 3. High school teachers —
  Australia. I. Title

373.11'02

Library of Congress Catalog Card Number: 84-72495

Printed by Macarthur Press, Australia

To three good teachers
Margaret Connell, Madge Dawson, Jean Blackburn

Contents

Introduction

This book is an account of the work of a number of secondary school teachers, the social relationships and structures that surround them, and the ways these relationships affect what they do as teachers. Its main purpose is to contribute to a difficult but strategic debate about social inequality and the future of public schooling. I hope also it may help explain teachers' working lives to other people, including parents of school students, and trainee teachers; and help practising teachers reflect on their own situations and purposes.

It arises from a project I undertook with Sandra Kessler, Gary Dowsett and Dean Ashenden on social differences in secondary schooling. In 1977-78 we interviewed 100 Year 9 and Year 10 students of differing class backgrounds in Sydney and Adelaide, together with their mothers and fathers and 128 of their teachers. Our main conclusions about the interactions among pupils, schools, and families as sources of social inequalities in education were published in 1982 in the book *Making the Difference* and the booklet *Ockers and Disco-maniacs*.

Those reports made very limited use of our interviews with teachers; but we were already convinced of their importance for a full understanding of the original problems. At the end of *Making the Difference* we wrote:

> Our argument must ultimately focus on their situation and their problems... It becomes very important, then, to get accurate bearings on the social situation of teachers, the constraints they work under, and the possibilities open to them

and promised some further research. This is it.

We had hoped to write, jointly, a longer and more ambitious book. The plan was to place a social analysis of teachers and

1

teaching in the context of the recent history of schooling and a detailed analysis of current educational policy issues, as well as offering a reformation of research and of teachers' relationships to the production of knowledge. That project got to the stage of detailed chapter outlines, some first drafts, and a title: *Lasting the Distance*. The preparatory work, the writing-up and discussion of case histories, debating of concepts and literature, and testing of ideas with teachers at in-service seminars and conferences, was done collectively by the four members of the research group.

For a number of reasons that joint plan went no further. This book is one member's attempt to make sense of the material the research group produced, focussed on a more limited set of themes and problems. It is more of a research report and less of an argument about current issues. If teachers find it of use, as I hope they may, it will mainly be in reflection. It is also more personal than the joint project, as its themes undoubtedly reflect some of my own puzzles and preoccupations. But while making this clear, I would also stress that the analysis is based on the work of the research group as a whole. What insights the book has to offer come mainly out of that collective process. When 'we' is written in the text it means the research group specifically; otherwise I write 'I'.

The 'new sociology of education' that emerged in the 1970s made giant strides with problems like the schools' relation to the economy, and the class bases of educational knowledge, but had curiously little to say about teachers. In the most influential text of the decade, Bowles and Gintis' *Schooling in Capitalist America*, teachers hardly figure as a problem at all; they were assumed to be more or less well-controlled agents of the capitalist system. In many other writings teachers were treated as vehicles of social control and therefore of little interest in themselves. Social analysis was mainly a matter of finding out what stood behind them. In the late 1970s, however, teachers were coming back into researchers' focus, especially in England. Grace's *Teachers, Ideology and Control* explored the social position of inner-city teachers and the social construction of the 'good teacher'; Woods' *The Divided School* offered a close-up picture of the 'hidden pedagogy of survival' and the underside of staffroom life. This interest seems to be continuing, as suggested by Barton and Walker's *Schools, Teachers and Teaching*. So does an older tradition of social-psychological research on teachers' socialisation and their professional and personal identity.

This study, therefore, may contribute to a general revival of interest in teachers as key actors in the social processes affecting education. It may also help develop our understanding of these processes in certain ways. First, it emphasises teachers' labour process as a point of departure for a wide range of problems. Second, it takes gender relations to be as important as class relations in the shaping of education and the lives of teachers. Third, it tries to bring together three levels of analysis which have, for the most part, remained separate: the personal life-history, the institutional life of the school, and large-scale social structures and dynamics.

The basis of the argument is the interviews already mentioned. As with the students and parents discussed in *Making the Difference*, we thought it essential to understand the teachers on their own terms before attempting to generalise. Accordingly we began by working up detailed case studies of individual teachers. Over the period from May 1980 to January 1983 we wrote, and then criticised and reconsidered, thirty-seven case studies. As themes, common patterns and new problems emerged, we wrote working papers and interpretative essays, sometimes incorporated into fresh case studies. The final stage was abstracting the analysed case studies into a grid of issues and problems. This was done in January 1984, and is the basis of the later parts of the book.

Given the rule of confidentiality under which this research was done, we did not feel entitled to print actual biographies, even with names, dates and places changed. Yet as we worked through the evidence it seemed more and more important, for readers' understanding of the social processes we were studying, to convey in the published report the *sense* of biography, the way things hang together and take shape (and sometimes fall out of shape) in teachers' lives. As a slightly uneasy compromise I have settled for constructing composite biographies, which are presented in Part One. Every detail in them comes from the interviews, but they come in each chapter from more than one. 'Terry Petersen', 'Rosa Marshall' and the others are therefore not real people. But I think reading chapters 1-5 as if they were, will give more insight into the lives of the actual teachers from whom the evidence comes than would a topic-by-topic, cross-sectional presentation of the same evidence. As a final precaution I have kept out of these accounts some of the more intimate and possibly painful material that many teachers told us about.

The second part of the book develops an industrial sociology of teachers, at least that part of an industrial sociology that concerns the workplace, the labour process, and the social relations of work. (Teacher unionism and 'industrial relations' on the system-wide scale were outside our research focus, though they are of course important.) These chapters go into some detail about what teaching feels like, i.e. the experience, but ultimately my concern is with what teachers actually do, i.e. the practice, and why they do it.

This provides a basis for the discussion in Part Three of teachers as a social group and as a force in educational politics. The issues here range from the ways teachers' social identity is constructed, through the ways their views of the world and education are constructed, to their part in the dynamics of gender, class, and educational reform. These are in no sense separate issues, nor are they ultimately separable from the issues of Part Two. It is clear from the analysis that relations of class and gender are embedded in the curriculum; it follows that reform of the curriculum is itself, in some measure, a reconstitution of these structures. The doctrine that tells teachers the schools are captive to capitalism and exhorts them to get on with the revolution outside, could not be more mistaken; it is teachers' work as teachers that is central to the remaking of the social patterns investing education.

As evidence for the understanding of teachers in general, our material has strengths and weaknesses. It is, as far as I know, unique among studies of teachers in having equal detail about students and parents, as well as being concerned with schools as institutions. We thus have considerable knowledge of the contexts of these teachers' working lives, the situations they are facing, and the social roots of their pedagogical problems. The study is also unusual in having interview material that allows the analysis to range from the personal level to social structures on the very large scale. Sociological studies have tended to ignore the personal dimensions of teaching and often give an oddly inhuman account of this most human of jobs; while psychological studies have even more resolutely ignored the question of where their problems come from.

At the same time the research design has two main drawbacks. First, because so much of our time went into the study of the pupils' families, our interviews with teachers were less thorough and less consistent than they ideally would be. Second, the sampling frame was intended to identify pupils' families; the teachers we interviewed were simply those who were teaching the girls and boys chosen in our sample and agreed to talk to us. Strictly speaking this cannot be taken as a representative sample of any well–defined population of teachers. Yet the procedure should guarantee a fair diversity within the secondary-teaching world, and has indeed done so. We have teachers from private schools and state schools (though not Catholic systemic schools); men and women in about equal numbers; the full range of subjects from mathematics to manual arts; classroom teachers from raw newcomers to old salts; and a scattering of department heads, deputies and principals. One can be reasonably confident that the processes analysed here are at least common ones. The response from the hundreds of teachers to whom we have presented parts of this argument over the past four years, and who have recognised many of their own experiences in it, provides some confirmation.

I should also stress, since the relationships discussed here are historical, that the interviews were done at a particular time. Some things have changed on the education scene in the six years we have spent analysing the material. I do not apologise for the lag; this kind of work cannot be hurried without losing its point. It should be remembered, however, that the present tense of the book is the late 1970s, and readers may find it interesting to consider what has changed, and what has not, since then.

At various points in the text I have noted interesting connections with other research, and referred to sources with practical advice on problems being discussed. I have not tried to keep up a running commentary on the rest of the research literature, nor to spell out all the implications for social theory. This would have made the book inaccessible to many readers with an interest in the problems. Holt, in his splendid slash at educational research in *The Common Curriculum*, remarks:

> We are, after all, trying to see why research has so little influenced classroom practice, and one reason is the irrelevance or pitiful inadequacy of much of the stuff that is published.[1]

Another reason is that much research which is both relevant and good is written up in an awful academic jargon and a format which makes it inaccessible to practising teachers. Teachers mostly have too much on their hands already to spend time and energy decoding academics' mysteries. It is up to the researchers to make themselves available, if they want their findings to be put to work.

We took the same view in writing *Making the Difference*, one result being that it has been thought by some critics to be a-theoretical. I should therefore say that this book, like *Making the Difference*, is highly theoretical; though its theorising about structure and practice, patriarchy and capitalism, person and society, is embedded in the argument rather than stated abstractly. I have explored many of its themes as problems of general social theory in a book of essays called *Which Way Is Up?*, which might be consulted by anyone interested in the conceptual underpinnings of the argument in this book.

Acknowledgements

The project was mainly funded by the Education Research and Development Committee (a body later abolished by cost-cutting ministers more concerned for share-markets than schools), and by the Macquarie University Research Committee. Funds were also granted by Sturt CAE (now the Sturt Campus of SACAE), Kuring-gai CAE, and the Society for the Production of Really Useful Knowledge. Permissions were granted by the NSW and SA Departments of Education, and by the principals of all schools involved in the study, state and Independent.

My main acknowledgements are to my co-workers Gary Dowsett, Dean Ashenden and Sandra Kessler, the scale of whose contribution has already been described; and to the teachers, students and parents who gave us interviews, some of them lengthy and difficult.

Other people have contributed in different ways. A project like this means an enormous amount of typing, much of it intricate and specialised. For a number of years the bulk of it was done, with extraordinary skill and speed, by Heather Williams when secretary to the Sociology discipline at Macquarie University. I am grateful also for the typing of manuscripts done by Helen Easson, Cynthia Hamilton, Jenny Bennett, Jann Kennedy, Judy Lain, Mary Gibbons and Mary Phillips. While working on this project I was stimulated and helped by discussions of teachers and schooling with three PhD students with whom I worked as supervisor, Carol O'Donnell, Lin Samuel and Michaela Anderson. The perspective on industrial sociology in Part Two reflects a great deal I have learnt from Gerry Phelan about labour, work places, and their political-economic contexts. Over a long period my ideas about schools and education have been shaped by those of my father, Bill Connell. In particular I have learnt from his concern for the nuts-and-bolts practicalities of schooling as well as grand ethical and cultural issues, and his sense that they can and should be brought together. Finally I am grateful to Michael Young and the Sociology of Education Department at the Institute of Education in London, for the setting in which the last stages of this work were done; and for hospitality and friendship to Robyn Dasey, in whose house most of the text was written.

Pam Benton has supported and enriched the work from beginning to end; in fact from before the beginning, as she helped shape the perspective out of which the study came. An involvement so constitutive is beyond ordinary thanks. I will simply say that this work, like the rest of my life, would hardly be conceivable without her.

Note on the text

The inset quotations are transcriptions of tape-recorded interviews, edited to remove the hesitations and repetitions of ordinary speech, and sometimes with intervening statements on other topics deleted. Interviewers' questions are shown in italics. All names of people and places in the study have been changed. References in Parts Two and Three to the composite case studies of Part One, and quotations under their names, relate to the interviews used in preparing the composites. Most of the text is written in the present tense; past tense is used when it seems appropriate to stress the particular time at which the interviews were done. It would be tiresome to write 'secondary teachers' all the time, though the point is made often enough that the discussion is about high schools and secondary colleges. Where 'teachers' and 'teaching' are written, 'secondary' is usually implied. Some features of the situations discussed are specific to secondary teaching, such as the link between school and labour market, the implications of adolescent sexuality, and the way high schools are time-tabled. Yet other parts, and perhaps more fundamental parts, of the story told here apply also to primary and tertiary teaching. I would think this generally true of the relationship of teachers' lives to their work, and also of much of what is argued about the labour process of teaching, about its emotional dimensions, about power relations in and around schools, about the school as a workplace, and about teachers' ideas and political practices. In this sense the argument about 'teaching' is appropriately phrased in the more general terms.

Note on 'class' and 'gender'

No-one can talk seriously about the social relationships involved in schooling without having some way of referring to social class on the one hand, gender and sexuality on the other. Yet there is no agreement, among social scientists or anyone else, about how to name or how to understand these matters. I should therefore briefly explain the usage in this book.

'Class relations' means the set of relationships between people and groups which centre on property, wealth, the employment relation and the labour market as a means of organising the society's production of resources and deciding their distribution. The 'working class' means, broadly, people who depend for a living on a wage or a wage substitute (like the dole or a pension); and the institutions (such as trade unions), social movements, and ways of life that have grown up around that situation. The 'ruling class' means people who own or control significant accumulations of wealth (mainly in companies) and thus act as employers of substantial numbers of workers, and people who through professional monopolies (e.g. lawyers, accountants) or organisational power (e.g. through the state) can appropriate comparable shares of the social product; together with the institutions (companies, clubs, private schools, cultural organisations, etc) that organise their power and their way of life. The families discussed in this book certainly do not represent a complete cross-section of either of these classes, but do stand for significant parts of them.

'Gender relations' means the set of social relations that organise sexuality and gender. This includes the sexual division of labour, the power relations between men and women, and between different groups within each sex (e.g. between heterosexual and homosexual people), institutions like the family, the social relations of childrearing, and the social movements and political struggles connected with issues such as sexual morality, the family, abortion rights, violence against women, gay rights, and the policing of sexuality. One's sex is so easily thought of as a purely biological matter that it often requires a real shift of perspective to think of this sphere of life in terms of social relations. That is, however, essential in understanding how social institutions such as schools operate.

More extended discussions of these concepts, and the problems of defining and using them, will be found in chapter 1 of *Class Structure in Australian History* (Connell and Irving, in bibliography), and the book of essays already mentioned, *Which Way is Up*?

Note for overseas readers on Australian education

The Australian school system is broadly similar to those of North America and Western Europe. It was historically based on British and American models, and has kept in close touch with developments in the North Atlantic world. It has however some local peculiarities which may need explaining.

The basic form of educational provision is a system of publicly funded schools, divided between primary (ages c.5–11) and secondary (ages c.12–18). These are in principle free (and in practice nearly so) and open to all. They account for about four-fifths of all school enrolments, and a very high percentage of working-class enrolments. I call these schools 'public' or 'state' schools in the text.

They are administered by the Education Departments of the six states and the two territories, aided by some funding from the federal government. These were established by the secular education reforms of the late nineteenth century colonial governments. They became notoriously bureaucratic organisations, providing a standardised elementary education for a widely-scattered population, training their own teachers and requiring them to adhere to fixed syllabuses. Travelling Inspectors of Schools were the main agents of rigid central control. In recent decades there has been a marked relaxation of central authority, closely connected with a massive growth of departmental secondary schools and a multiplication of universities and other tertiary institutions outside departmental control. The Department of Education still remains the centre of educational affairs in each state. Its administrative head is the Director General of

Education, responsible to the Minister of Education in the state government of the day.

Public schools are mainly organised on an area basis. A network of local primary schools serves urban neighbourhoods and country towns. Before World War II the public system provided limited secondary schooling, mainly in sex-segregated vocational junior-secondary schools and a few highly selective university-oriented grammar schools. In all states there was a massive growth of secondary enrolments through the 1950s and after (peaking about 1977). This boom was accompanied by a major institutional reform that created a network of co-educational comprehensive (i.e. non-selective) high schools, each taking the whole output of the 'feeder' primary schools in its area. These schools are now the basic form of secondary education provision in Australia, and are the main subject of this book. (The public system still contains a smaller number of selective and vocational —for example agricultural, technical—schools in patterns that vary from state to state.)

One-fifth of enrolments are in non-government schools. Most of these are in Roman Catholic systemic schools, administered by the church but now almost wholly funded by the government, and taught by lay staff with curricula and methods that closely follow those of the government schools. They are not included in this study. The remaining enrolments are in private or Independent schools. Much the most influential of these are the mainly Protestant colleges started in the colonial era on the model of the English 'public schools' to provide secondary education for the children of colonial gentry and merchants. These spawned feeder primary schools (often still called 'prep'—for preparatory—schools) and have remained the principal form of schooling for the children of the wealthy through large changes in the composition of the Australian ruling class. These 'high-fee private', 'elite private' schools or 'colleges' are the private schools mainly discussed in the text. They now get substantial government funding but also have significant income from fees and endowments.

The third 'tier' of the education system is entirely government funded: Universities, Colleges of Advanced Education, Institutes of Technology, etc. Teacher training for the state system used to be done mainly in single purpose departmental Teachers' Colleges. It is now partly located in the universities, and partly in multi-purpose Colleges of Advanced Education (themselves often former Teachers' Colleges that have become autonomous). The younger state school teachers discussed in this book have mainly been trained at universities, doing a year's full-time study of education and teaching method (the Diploma of Education, universally called the 'DipEd') at the end of three years of undergraduate work for a BA or BSc majoring in a 'teaching subject' such as history or mathematics. In some places the DipEd is taught concurrently with the bachelor's degree, and in some places by correspondence.

Entry to tertiary education is mainly regulated by a set of competitive examinations taken at the end of secondary schooling, about the age of eighteen. The detail and the name varies from state to state and from time to time; for simplicity I call all versions 'Matric' in the text. Only a minority of students in the state and Catholic school system actually last to the Matric. The majority leave by age seventeen after four years of secondary schooling. There is generally an examination or certification at this stage too, the form of which varies considerably from state to state. I refer to this certification as the 'School Certificate'.

The pupils discussed in the book are from Year 9 (average age: 14.5 years) and Year 10 (average age: 15.5 years)—i.e. the final years of compulsory schooling.

A few other details about Australian affairs may need explaining. The federal government at the time of the interviews was a conservative coalition headed as Prime Minister by Malcolm Fraser, a wealthy grazier from Victoria. The Liberal Party is the main conservative force, a business-based party analogous to the Progressive Conservative Party in Canada and the Conservative Party in Britain. The federal opposition, now the government, was the Labor Party, a union-based party analogous to Labour in Britain and the Social Democratic party in Sweden.

Though the Australian economy depends heavily on mineral and agricultural exports it is also substantially industrialised. Two companies are mentioned in the text: BHP (Broken Hill Proprietary), the largest manufacturing and mining company in the country; and General Motors, the US corporation whose Australian subsidiary is the largest local vehicle manufacturer. The international recession of the mid and late 1970s had a sharp impact on Australian manufacturing, resulting in widespread unemployment in the cities where this study was done.

1

Sheila Goffman and Margaret Blackall

This chapter introduces two teachers in working-class high schools. Both are young and both are teaching in academic areas of the curriculum, but they have already evolved very different teaching styles.

The schools they work in are comprehensive high schools in the state system. One is on the urban fringe, a product of recent expansion—one pupil's father reminisced about shooting rabbits in the paddock where the school was later built. The other is in an older-established suburb but still well out from the city centre. Both have substantially working-class clienteles. Fathers work as storemen, carpenters, railway shunters and so on; mothers as cleaners, packers, sometimes clerks, and of course houseworkers. There are some families of small business people and public servants, not too many. On the other hand there are few in dire poverty; there are no transients in these areas, and almost everyone lives in a one-family bungalow with a bit of land for a garden. Some families are renting from the Housing Authority, some are buying houses on long time-payment, some bought a block of land and have built their own. There is the ethnic mixture that is usual in the Australian working class nowadays, but not a high migrant population in either neighbourhood. English is much the commonest language at home and virtually the only language spoken in the playground. There is some unemployment among the adults, especially the women, and serious unemployment among young people.

Being a teacher

Sheila Goffman, only two years out from university, is quite possibly the most popular teacher in her school. She is a pro-

13

gressive teacher in the child-centred vein, who is making a raging success of it in an unlikely setting.

It was not done smoothly. She had wanted to be a teacher from early in her own high school years, and the academically-oriented state school she went to launched her easily enough into university. Nor did she have much trouble getting her Bachelor of Arts degree, or her Diploma of Education. She was offered a job immediately by the Education Department, and came straight to Rockwell High. That was where the trouble hit.

The school is not exceptionally rough, but it has problems of control. The kids walked all over her. In retrospect she is critical of her teacher training. It gave her lots of ideas for lessons,

> but I was never prepared for the discipline, at all. I think it was unreal.

Facing the classic shock of the idealistic young teacher dumped into her first classroom, she reacted in a classic way. She came down hard on the kids. She called in support from the school hierarchy, and insisted on silence and order. After a few months she got it.

But she soon came to see this as the wrong solution. She had control, all right; but the kids still were not learning anything.

> Learning doesn't necessarily happen in a dead quiet classroom with everyone jumping when you say 'jump'.'

So she began to put her main effort into building personal relationships with the kids in which they *would* become involved.

This has led in two directions. On the one hand it has produced lively, informal classes with a great deal of student participation. Most of the kids love it. Sheila has gone far beyond the conventional devices of debates and projects. She has adapted encounter-group techniques, and uses them as 'self-exploration' exercises in the classroom. She uses workshops, self-directed group projects, and free-floating discussions in which she is an active participant but not the source of all wisdom. And this energy is by no means confined to the classroom. She is also involved with the school magazine and the drama programme, she supervises debating, organises the school dance, goes on vacation camps with the kids.

On the other hand she has tried to individualise the teaching.

Her view of education is based firmly on the idea of individual development. It is nicely summed up in her response to parents' views that school is for learning the basics. Yes, agrees Sheila, but it is more than that: 'they're here to grow up'. She tries to work out the appropriate tasks, but give to the kids the responsibility for doing them. She has a clear notion of the normal pattern of adolescent development, worries about any who depart from it, and tries to act according to the needs of each one. She has no hesitation about intervening in their peer relations for this purpose. For instance she tried to separate Greg Wilkins, a Year 9 boy in our sample, from a friend who she thought was holding him back in 'immature' behaviour.

Two things are obvious about this kind of teaching. First, to do it well requires a lot of time and energy. Sheila not only gives herself freely. Her relations with the kids obviously *generate* energy and stimulate her as a teacher. Still, however much energy there is, it is never enough. She too is bound by the facts of staff-student ratios and the school's limited and parcelled time. She notes for instance that Greg Wilkins, whom she thinks likely to leave school at Year 10, needs extra attention to solve his problems of shyness and poor written expression; and she cannot give it to him.

Second, this kind of pedagogy demands that the teacher get to know the students well at a personal level. Sheila is a mine of information about the kids' characters and situations, the different layers in their personality, the ups and downs of their relations with each other, their love lives, their hopes and fears. She is certainly a good practical psychologist, but it is more than that. She has taken the trouble to gather information about these things, in the classroom, in her other activities around the school, and even outside the school. She regularly drives kids home in her car, though she does not live in the district. And they, many of them, respond in kind. They talk to her about things they rarely confide to teachers, for instance sexual and family problems. They join in her programmes with curiosity, enthusiasm and, in the view of some other teachers, rather too much movement and noise.

Margaret Blackall is a language teacher at a school with a reasonably similar clientele, Greenway High. It is her first school and she has been there for six years. Her route into teaching was very similar to Sheila's: a selective state school, a university BA and DipEd, and straight into a Departmental appointment. And she had the same kind of experience at the jump. Her response was similar to Sheila Goffman's first response: to survive you have to get on top. But the emotional shading was slightly different:

After you have gone through the first year of teaching, you can organise yourself a bit better. You know what to expect, you care less what the kids think of you. In your first year out, you still treat them as monsters, or as you would treat any other adult. Now I treat kids more as I should treat them. I don't yell at them any more, or only rarely I suppose. And I like to cultivate a friendly but firm relationship with them, which I find works very well with most kids. A little bit like a big sister, but a strict big sister, who expects things.

Her solution, then, was not the about-face that Sheila did. It was to find balances: in relationships with the kids, a balance between friendliness and firmness; and in her own relationship with the job, a balance between caring and making herself too vulnerable.

The outcome of this search for balance is a teaching style that seems markedly more conventional. Margaret's classrooms are quiet and orderly; she insists on a degree of decorum that more free-floating staff see as even a shade authoritarian. Another teacher observed about her:

Very prim and proper, a very good teacher, but she expects them to behave as kids did about fifteen years ago. For instance, Jacko, this kid chews gum in class all the time. I think he's written his exercise book out a couple of times for her!

Margaret herself comments on how taut the classroom should be in relation to another of her classes, a small group studying for the School Certificate:

I've been a lot more lenient with them than I should be, because I know them so well. And I feel they've taken advantage, work-wise, and think 'Well she's a good old stick. She won't mind if we haven't done the homework'. And then I get very frustrated.

Her interactions with the kids thus are noticeably more formal and, as the jargon has it, 'teacher-centred' than is the case with Sheila Goffman. This corresponds to a somewhat different view of what education is about. She too explains it by means of an interesting contrast with parent's ideas:

For me, schools are to pass on knowledge, to make people grow intellectually, to civilise them, however you would like to see that process done. I don't really see them as job finders. I don't like utilitarian education. Perhaps that's too idealistic, but I feel that if you have grown as a person, you will find something. We shouldn't be sort of channelling people into boxes.

So Margaret shares with Sheila a notion of 'growth', and a distaste for making the school an agent of the labour market. But for her the notion of growth is much more about the growth of the mind, and teaching is above all the communication of knowledge in the cause of enlightenment.

For this goal she is prepared to work hard and long. She too is a dedicated teacher, who cares a great deal what happens to the kids. Sheila is more intimate with them, but nothing she says is quite as moving as Margaret's explanation of why she rejects the policy of streaming:

Here at this school, my very first day with the children having the tests, and then next day putting them into groups, and seeing the children sitting around. And straight away they knew which was the best group, which was the worst group. And hearing a little girl say that she hadn't been picked for any group yet: 'Oh, I hope I get in this group', and 'Oh, that must be the good group because such-and-such is in it'. And then the last group called out, and she was in it. The dejected way, on the second day of the school year, that she went to that class, knowing that it was the dummy class—that was dreadful. And for all the good things that go with streaming, I would never advocate it, because of that.

The trouble is, concern with intellect and knowledge normally implies a policy of streaming, and a notion that the kids' results on tests simply reflect their 'ability'. Margaret is too sensitive, and too clear-sighted, to swallow all of that uncritically. But the result is that she has to take the consequences of streaming on board as an emotional problem for herself; just as she had taken on board the School Certificate class's slackness about homework as if it were her own moral responsibility.

Sources and supports

Sheila Goffman is making a success of child-centred pedagogy in an environment where that would not normally happen. It is a crucial fact that she is not trying to do it alone. Her search for a teaching style in her first year took the turn it did partly because it met up with a reconstruction of her department's work being undertaken by a new subject head.

Like whole schools, individual departments are from time to time taken in hand by a new head and renovated. John Demetriou came to Rockwell High the year before Sheila. It is his first promotion position, and he has been energetic in introducing new ideas: individualised instruction, breaking down streaming, placing strong emphasis on 'relevance' and contemporary issues. He has campaigned for, and with the support of the principal won, funding for a specialised resources centre for his subject.

Sheila's interest in her students' development, and her social skills, dovetailed with John Demetriou's programme. She admires him, remarking that he really believes the kids come first and acts accordingly. The consequence is not only a warm reception for her flow of bright ideas about the curriculum, but also a context of support for her student-centred practices. The English staff as a group decided to throw open their staffroom to the kids to come in and chat, to convey the idea that they think of them as 'people' with whom one can have a relationship outside the classroom. Other departments, Sheila notes, think they are 'crazy' to give up their privacy—and, no doubt, create unwelcome precedents. The custom in the school is that the kids stop at the door and do not come into staffrooms.

Positive relations with her immediate colleagues, her department head, and more remotely the school principal (who has also supported her schemes) are plainly important in making Sheila the kind of teacher she is. But it is also a question of the kind of person she is. Talkative, confident, cheerful, but also sensitive to emotions and concerned with other people's responses to her. She is good with people, establishes contact easily. One of her Year 9 students has a talent for cartooning and drew a series of the Rockwell High teachers. He pictured Sheila as a hippie, with fuzzy hair, a big smile, an open mouth—and surrounded by kids.

There is another level to this, for the pattern is not just a matter of an outgoing style. It is also, quite specifically, a type of femininity. In some ways Sheila runs counter to traditional stereotypes of women. She is active, assertive, deeply involved in her career. Yet her personal version of progressive education, which stresses caring, sensitivity, and emotional relationships, can only be understood in the context of her femininity. It expresses something basic about the way she has been constituted as a person, and the way she has constituted herself. And it is an important reason for her difficulty in understanding the rather different patterns of femininity she is meeting among the Rockwell girls.

Margaret Blackall works in a department where the atmosphere is rather cooler, and no doubt this is one reason for her pedagogy having taken a different shape from Sheila's. But in understanding Margaret's teaching and her impact on the students at Greenway, we need to give closest attention to her own outlook. She is a more reserved and more self-sufficient person than Sheila, and has also put more effort into thinking out her educational philosophy.

When Margaret suggested, in the passage already quoted, that she put more stress on the importance of knowledge than the parents do, she was not making a rhetorical gesture. This is important to her. It is close to the heart of why she is a teacher, and why she has stayed a teacher despite the trauma of her first year and the emotional battering it has meant since.

> I'm here mostly because I love my subject so much. I want to instil a love of knowledge in general, I think. I want people to have the same sort of rewarding experience that I have.

In short, she feels herself to be an intellectual. And she feels intellectual life has a vital, though much under-rated, part to play in society as a whole. This view of knowledge gives a dignity to the teacher's task which Margaret feels, which informs her interested-but-firm relations with the kids—and which is undermined by teachers like Sheila.

Margaret is also committed to teaching as a career. She comes from a working-class family whose education was limited but all the more valued for that. She was a high flyer at school, and now sees teaching as a life-time career. She is going for her first promotion now; intends to take leave to travel overseas, then come back to the Department and look around for a transfer. She has a professional identity as a teacher, into which her view of the importance of knowledge is integrated.

For professional women there is a classic tension between having a career and being a wife-and-mother. Margaret faces this in a very direct form. She is married, and her husband has a different job and different interests.

I'm not the sort of person who says 'Come home for a Chinese meal, all of you'. I can't really, because my husband is not part of this life. He has nothing to do with teaching.
Do you think he understands the things you go through?
He does in a way, and he doesn't. He can't because he is not a teacher. He doesn't know the pressures, and his job has very little pressure. I can't keep up with his outside activities because I'm so tired and worn out.
Would he like you to give up teaching?
Not really. He knows I would be bored if I did. He thinks it would be a waste of my education. He knows that despite what I say, and how miserable I get and how I say it's a dreadful job, and I hate it, deep down I couldn't do without it.

But of course for married women there always *is* the culturally-honoured option of 'staying home' and having children. So whether she likes it or not, there always is a tension around Margaret's way of being a woman.

The interviews give some hints that getting on top of unruly classes and maintaining authority have required some suppression of her femininity; her friction with Jacko, the boy who chews in class, is a case in point. On the other hand she places as full a stress on *caring* for the kids as Sheila Goffman does, and has perhaps as much sensitivity to the emotional consequences of what happens in school, as illustrated by her reaction to the streaming of the new first-year class. Margaret has not got hardened. But she is certainly having to negotiate some awkward corners; and this helps produce her no-nonsense, occasionally brusque style with the kids.

Contexts

We favour 'teaching the individual', Sheila observes, while conservative staff favour 'teaching the class'. This is unfair to some of the conservatives in her school, but it certainly catches a central feature of her own approach to teaching. She has taken the individualising of instruction as the leading idea in John Demetriou's renovation programme. Like many other teachers she phrases the aims of education in terms of promoting individual growth; and her extensive personal knowledge of the kids *is* her professional knowledge, in this conception of the teaching profession.

There are some individuals for whom her high-energy approach is not working. We have mentioned her worry about young Greg Wilkins, who plainly needs remedial work which she cannot find the time to do. More troubling is that while her group methods work like a dream with some of the kids, others refuse to be involved. Her self-exploration exercises, for instance, find some kinds closing up, others clowning around, others pretending to be stupid. Even closer to home, Sheila finds that some of the kids simply do not want to open up to *her*, or relate to her in the one-to-one way that is central to an individualised pedagogy.

A case in point is Elaine Markham, a successful Year 9 student who could become one of the school's academic stars. Sheila is annoyed with her behaviour in the classroom, 'always giggling and chattering and off-the-air sort of thing'. Sheila experiences Elaine as 'superficial'; she feels there is another person below the surface, but cannot get to her. What is lurking below the surface, as we discovered when we interviewed Elaine and her parents at considerable length, is a fiercely complicated set of family tensions, many of them concerning schooling and economic advancement, that both fuel Elaine's engagement with her schoolwork and make it a source of tension and distress for her. She has worked out her ways of handling it, but they involve some awkward compromises and delicate balances. She has every reason for resisting Sheila's well-meant attempts to get her to open up and spill the beans.

Sheila's pedagogy, then, runs into trouble at the point where it encounters social forces which act on a scale beyond the one-to-one or small-group processes she revels in, and which cannot be understood in a framework of 'encouraging individual growth'. Sheila thinks she is failing to reach some of the kids. What she does not see is that her practices incorporate many but *exclude* others. And this incorporation and exclusion is not random. Her big successes are in the 'A' and 'B' streams of this streamed school. (It is a sign of the support she is getting that although a new teacher she is given mostly top-stream classes to teach.) The bottom streams are a different kettle of fish. The only hostile comment about kids she lets drop in the whole interview is when she talks about an immigrant boy, now doing exceptionally well in 9A, who had been put in 9F on his arrival; she sympathises with how he must have felt 'being down there with all the dodoes'. Margaret Blackall has a much clearer perception of how it feels to be labelled a 'dodo' by the school, and why 9F is the way it is.

We may suggest, then, that Sheila's success as a teacher, which is real enough and exciting for all concerned, is partly produced by the specific context in which it occurs. It seems that her pedagogy works specifically with kids who already have had some academic success and who are happy with the school, or at least do not resent being there.

Towards the end of the interview she begins to talk in a way that brings such issues nearer to the surface. Her close contact with kids means that she learns something, even if at second hand, about the circumstances they live in. Her own adolescence had been an unquestioning progress along a well-marked-out path.

> Here, the kids just don't know what's going to happen to them. Some of the Year 8 kids are leaving to work. They've just turned 15, and they're going off and they've got nothing. Nothing at all. And you ask any number of them what they're going to do and they say, 'Oh, I'll have to go on the dole'. That's the saddest thing for them, but it's true. That's all there is for them, because they're not going to move away from here. And that was a thing that never crossed my mind when I was at school, and never crossed my friends' minds. We just accepted that if we were in the A or B or C class we would go right through to Matric and we'd go to university.

So she has been learning from the kids some uncomfortable facts: about mass youth unemployment, about the search for jobs, about unwanted pregnancies, about being trapped in the working-class suburb. At the edge of her mind Sheila is beginning to formulate some rather different educational problems, about teaching for survival, about ways the kids can share their experience of the labour market. But so far these have not come into focus. Individual growth remains very much the centre of her thinking.

For this reason, also, she has not made much contact with the parents. Her popularity with the kids is not reproduced among their parents, some of whom, indeed, are highly critical of her. She is aware of this, and aware of some of its roots. She observes of parents and teachers

> The difference is not that we don't come from a working–class
> background, because some of us do. The difference is in the
> education we've had.

And she accurately notes of the parents, 'I think a lot of them
must have hated school themselves'—an important fact, recognised by few of the teachers we spoke to. What she does not see
is that many working–class parents still have a great respect for
education and knowledge, and themselves have knowledge and
resources that the school could build on. Sheila declares herself
in favour of more parent involvement, but it is clear this is to be
on the teachers' terms. Parents can for instance come and help
paint the new resources centre. The simple truth is that parents
do not impinge much on Sheila's work, and she has not had to
think hard about them.

Margaret Blackall is one of the teachers who do 'come from a
working–class background'. Neither of her parents got past First
Year at high school. Her father is a transport worker; her
mother had unskilled and temporary jobs as a factory hand and
a waitress before getting married and becoming a full-time
housewife. There was never much money about.

> School was a different world, that's all. We didn't have books at
> home. I didn't join a library until I was 14.

But this did *not* mean that her parents had different values
from the school, or failed to support her education. Margaret
points this out while reading a vehement lesson to educational
sociologists:

> They were lower class. They had to be, because of the money that
> was coming in. But their values were the same as what I had at
> school: you shouldn't steal, you weren't supposed to smoke, you
> had to be a decent sort of person. There was no contradiction
> whatever. In fact I would say my family were a lot stricter than
> some. And my mother would always see the school as right, I
> would always be wrong, if there was any question.
> *Do you think your experience is different from a lot of teachers?*
> Yes, it is. I found that at college when I did sociology I felt very
> resentful of some of the things that were said.
> *What sort of things?*
> Well, when they made sweeping generalisations about lower class
> and middle class. I still think 'middle-class morality', what else do

you replace it with? It might be 'middle-class morality', but I see it as the only force under which civilisation can go on and live.

Here is another source of Margaret's conception of teaching and her relations with her working-class pupils; she is faithfully reproducing her mother's approach to her.

Margaret is far more socially and politically aware than Sheila. She knows that class relations are not just a question of the workers being different; she comments on the concentration of wealth and power in Australian society, and has a good grasp of party politics and its social bases. She has carefully thought out views on issues such as homosexuality and abortion, uranium mining, racism, poverty. She would like to see more support for the poor, and more equality generally. She is aware of how education divides working-class people. She is sharply critical of policies such as streaming and the use of IQ tests. She would like to see the school opening the kids' eyes more. She is, in short, an articulate and thoughtful progressive on a whole range of social and educational issues.

One of the issues that concerns her is the position of women at Greenway High. It is a school where all the senior staff (subject department heads and administration) are men, with only one exception. Attempts to have this changed have met with no success. The senior staff in general, Margaret says bluntly, are 'male chauvinist pigs'. A woman can fit in by accepting the patronage of men. Margaret Blackall, like some others of her colleagues, is too tough-minded and independent to accept such a definition of women's place. The result over the past few years has been a good deal of friction and not very much progress; it is one of the reasons she will be looking for a transfer to another school. She would like schooling to do something positive to advance the interests of the girls.

The trouble with this, as with her view that education should advance working-class interests, is in how it is done. Her commitment to academic teaching, and the rather formal relationship she constructs with her pupils, leaves her with little means of influencing the kids' fates except helping promote some individuals up the academic (and perhaps occupational) ladder. As most cannot climb this ladder, the way it is set up now, her strategies are ultimately as divisive as Sheila's.

Sheila has no such consciousness of the facts of power, and has a much more favourable relationship with the men who hold authority in her school. Nevertheless her close interaction with the kids makes it impossible for her to miss the sexism that permeates their everyday lives. She notes that the Year 9 boys are constantly experimenting with dirty language, that the Year 9 girls never sit down with the boys if they can help it, and so on. But she almost always sees the kids' sexual lives in terms of one-to-one relations and in terms of their relative 'maturity', not in terms of larger social patterns.

She tells the story of a bright girl in her class last year who had to leave because she got pregnant. Sheila asked her why she had not used contraception, and got the classic answer: she had not intended to fuck, so did not take precautions. Of course the boy did not either, but no one focussed on that. The point is that Sheila is exasperated with the girls for not going on the pill, and tries to persuade them to be 'a little more realistic'; that is, more like her.

Contraception is compatible with her form of femininity; she cannot grasp the kind of femininity in which it would be destructive to admit in advance that you are 'that kind of girl'. The dimension of sexual power in working-class adolescent life —the unending harassment of the girls, the problems of creating and maintaining a reputation, the boys' struggle to establish masculinity in the context of their own class and ethnic subordination—never comes into focus.

Both class and gender relations, then, are throwing up problems which impinge on these teachers' work in powerful ways, and which neither of their approaches seems to be resolving. The teachers' dilemma in the face of such problems is nowhere more poignantly put than in Margaret Blackall's description of one of her encounters. There is a good deal of friction in her school on ethnic lines, a good deal of racial prejudice. She was speaking to one of the Greek boys:

> I was very much concerned and hurt because he said to me that all his teachers were just Anglo-Saxon bastards and had no under-standing of how they felt. And I sat down and talked to him, and I said 'Look, I'm really hurt about that, because here I am trying to promote another language at school'. I said 'I'm not Anglo–Saxon anyway, not really, because I've got about seven or

eight different strains'. I said 'So don't say that, because it's not true'. I said that I was really hurt and—
How did he handle that?
Well, he sort of said 'I don't mean you anyway'. But you wondered if he didn't say that so he could leave and stop this talk.

2

Terry Petersen

Terry Petersen is the senior technical teacher at Rockwell High. He is in his late thirties, and has spent nearly ten years at this school. He is in fact one of its longest-serving staff, and is very well informed about how it works and what its problems are. As the head of the Manual Arts department he has administrative work to do, but tries to minimise this. He sees himself as basic-ally a classroom teacher, and views the world of education very much from this perspective.

Teaching as a path in life

Terry has been in teaching a lot longer than Sheila Goffman and Margaret Blackall, and for him it has the shape of a life project. He came in along a different route. He grew up in a mining town, his father being a carpenter and his mother, as is usual in such towns, a full-time housewife. He remembers the local public schools as having been good—the town demanded it—but like most of the boys he left school at 14 and went down the mine. The difference was that he already had in mind the idea of further education, and needed to save for it. While working, he got a trade ticket as a carpenter.

Some years later he decided to became a teacher. The actual decision was quite sudden, though it had been maturing for a long time. He looked up the address of the Department of Education in the telephone book, went in and declared his interest in becoming a teacher, and filled in the form they gave him. Four weeks later, in best Departmental fashion, he received a printed notice telling him to report to the Teachers College for a three-year training course.

This was in the days of the teacher shortage, and Terry does not set great store by his selection, remarking

It wasn't long ago, you were just warm and erect, and you were a teacher.

Nevertheless it represented a real social promotion for a boy from the mines, with consequences that have continued to ramify through his life. In the meantime, his years of practical experience in hard conditions counted for nothing. Regulations required him to do basic training again: he had to 'learn' to plane a piece of timber! It was only later, when a school needed a qualified tradesman for a teaching job, that he could claim credit for his trade. Understandably, Teachers College does not occupy a warm place in his memories. But he got the hang of the teaching trade, too, and moved on into the schools.

His career in the Department has been along standard lines. The first appointment was to a small and very remote country school, of the kind made famous by the film and book *Wake In Fright*. Surviving that, he moved to appointments in country towns, where he was able to make use of his trade, and thence back to the city as a senior technical teacher. Rockwell High is his fifth school, and the one where he has felt most comfortable and settled. In fact he moved house to Rockwell not long after getting this posting, and is possibly the only member of the teaching staff (as distinct from the clerical, cleaning and caretaking staff) who actually lives in the school's catchment area.

Terry comes from a social background which is quite like that of the families whose kids he teaches at Rockwell High. They are, as well, his neighbours. He *knows*, or at least he feels he knows, what they are like. Yet his occupation sets him apart. There are very few people in this suburb who have anything like three years of higher education. The conditions of his work are significantly different from those in the factories, warehouses and shops where most of Rockwell's adults earn their daily bread. Terry's fellow teachers usually place a certain distance between themselves and the milieu they have to work in.

The result is to make Terry highly sensitive to issues of class, and very mixed in his reactions. On the one hand he is proud of his manual skills and his knowledge of the real world of industry. He is a solid supporter of the teachers' union, indeed calls himself 'a bloody-minded unionist', and gives his mining-town origins credit for that. On the other hand he is clear that teachers are not like ordinary workers, that they are 'middle class' and should not be ashamed to admit it. In Terry's perception the difference between classes is largely educational, and he is sharply critical of the attitudes to education he sees among much of the school's clientele:

> Do I have to be honest? I'm probably a snob, you see. The difference is that when somebody worked hard for something, they earned it, they appreciate it. Somebody who's been given something in most cases doesn't look after it... The parents don't hold the school in esteem. For the life of me, I don't know why.

This sort of tension is familiar enough, not only among teachers. In Terry's life, however, there is an extra twist of the knife. It is not just a question between the school and the parents, but also an issue within the school. He is a manual arts teacher in an institution where academic knowledge holds pride of place; and that is not always an easy situation.

Being a technical teacher

Terry is in the classroom 24 periods a week, teaching. (The 24 periods are face-to-face; there is in addition, preparation time and marking time, as well as his work as a subject senior.) The differents in his situation start with what happens in his classroom.

In recent years there has been something of a curriculum revolution in the 'practical' subjects. What used to be a steady diet of woodwork-and-metalwork for the boys, cooking-and-sewing for the girls, has diversified into a broader manual-arts programme. The materials now include leather, enamel, ceramics, plastics, etc. And the conception of what the subject is about has been enlarged, with 'technical drawing', for instance, being expanded to 'graphic communication', and courses on materials introduced that give an elementary view of engineering problems. New media have been included: some schools have photography courses now, and some are taking up video and computing.

All this has affected Rockwell High. The current principal wants to modernise, and has approved the diversification that Terry Petersen and the other technics staff have been attempting. But the resources have not been there. The workshop space is severely limited; it was designed for a smaller intake, and never upgraded. The staff available have also been too few, with a staff:student ratio of 1:20, about 25 per cent worse than the recommended ratio in manual arts. They have not been able to buy sophisticated equipment on the normal school budget, and Rockwell is not quite poor enough to qualify for Disadvantaged Schools Programme funds. The result is a time-tabling nightmare, to get all the kids through in a week, and serious restrictions on the new materials and topics. In practice Terry spends most of his time teaching his own trade, woodwork.

In the classroom he has easy, though firmly didactic, relations with the kids. He moves around the room a lot, talking to individual students, and often giving specific tuition in skills as students work on their individual jobs. At regular intervals he reverts to talk-and-chalk with the whole class in order to explain principles, talk about materials, and so forth, but this never dominates his teaching.

Terry reports none of the horrendous problems of control that teachers of academic subjects like Sheila Goffman and Margaret Blackall have encountered with the same kids. Of course he is much more experienced than Sheila or Margaret, he is a man, and he carries more weight in the school. But the manual-arts teachers we interviewed generally seem to have easier relations with the kids, and it is worth considering what it is about their classrooms that might have this effect. The guts of it is that the kids like being there. In the first place there are fewer of them. Safety considerations alone dictate small numbers in a workshop, so every kid is likely to get some individual attention regularly. Secondly, the lessons themselves have an inbuilt informality. With teacher and pupil doing the same hands-on task side by side, formal hierarchy is hard to maintain. This is not to say there is no control: far from it. Terry controls his classes in a thoroughly teacher-centred way. The point is that when he tells the kids what to do, he is acting on the authority of skills and knowledge they readily recognise and respect. For the most part they jump to it *and* like it.

Thirdly, more than in most classrooms, the students have their own individual tasks to work at, and can do them more or less at their own pace. Terry constantly talks about a pupil's 'job', a term widely used for a task in the technics area and never for an English essay or a History assignment. And finally, as this term itself suggests, there is a direct element of practical usefulness in what is done. Often the project itself—a sugar-scoop, a book-end, a pendant, a skirt—can be immediately used, shown to parents and friends, and thus socially validated. The kids commonly believe they are learning skills they can use when they leave school and go to work. (Terry himself does not think so.)

The bottom line is that, with the possible exception of sport, manual arts are the most popular subjects at Rockwell High—with the kids. That is almost the exact opposite of their position on the prestige hierarchy among teachers. The academic subjects associated with university, and especially the more prestigious university faculties, still carry most clout. Among the 'electives', languages are high status and technics are low. Terry knows this, his colleagues know it, the kids know it. To some extent this has a positive effect, creating fellow-feeling in the manual arts staffroom and even some solidarity with students. But for the most part it is a source of frustration. They might get more of the equipment they need if the subjects they taught counted for more in the school's scheme of things. The technics teachers even face the indignity of having to dun the kids for their extra fees (the students' families have to pay for materials used), a point Terry is bitter about, but has not been able to change. Terry must expect to lose most of his best students. He cannot press them to keep on with manual arts, as he knows that their own best interest, in terms of promotion through the education system, usually lies in going for the high-prestige electives. So one of teaching's great rewards, seeing the flowering of a pupil's work to a high level of skill, is often denied him.

The subject he teaches, then, sharpens the personal politics of class that Terry has had to negotiate in his own life. Terry has made a deliberate and deep commitment to the profession of teaching. He has identified himself with the collective interest of teachers through his unionism. He has taken on their social identity, distancing himself from his own roots to do so. He puts effort and thought not only into his classroom work and his department, but also into general educational questions.

But an alignment with teachers-in-general means inevitably a commitment to their professional identity, which is centred on the body of knowledge that teachers control and promote, the knowledge with which Margaret Blackall identifies so deeply. At this period of history, that means above all academic knowledge organised in the hierarchical, competitive way the testing and selection system requires. A curriculum dominated by that kind of knowledge inevitably marginalises Terry Petersen's work as a manual arts teacher, whatever gloss of 'free-choice-of-electives' or 'educate-the-whole-person' the system tries to put on it. So he protests. But because his own professional identity is bound up with the educational regime that is doing this, his protests are muted, or focus on specifics, or get converted into sardonic humour. Given this situation, there is no way he can win.

Kids, parents, jobs

That should not suggest Terry is a sour, frustrated chalkie. Quite the contrary, he is an energetic person with good relations with the kids and an important role in the school. There are lots of pluses in the job. Among other things the informal character of the carpentry classes means he talks a lot with the kids and gets to know them on a personal level rather better than most teachers.

One consequence of this is a clear perception of gender processes. Terry went to a single-sex school himself, and does not really agree with coeducation; segregated classes, he thinks, give better results. To support this argument he points out that sexual segregation occurs by choice:

Nobody [no teacher] pressures and selects subject choice in electives. We leave it up to the kids, with the guidance of their parents.

The result is predictable: massive segregation, especially in the manual arts area. Only one boy in Year 9, for instance, is doing home science along with the girls, and he has constantly to defend himself against the imputation of being a queer: 'if anybody suggested different he'd thump them. He's not a little fellow'. A few girls do metalwork and woodwork, not many. Only one Year 8 girl is doing graphic communication (formerly 'technical drawing') among all the boys, and is probably only sustained in it by the fact that she is coming top. Some of the newer areas, like leatherwork and ceramics, have a more mixed clientele.

On the face of it, this segregation is against the interests of the manual arts department. Staffing is allocated in relation to student numbers, and the case for equipment funding and more space would also be strengthened if the numbers grew. It would therefore make sense for manual arts teachers to encourage both girls and boys to choose the electives which gender conventions

currently freeze them out of. Terry is aware of this. Yet there is
little encouragement for it to happen, except in cases of unusual
talent.

One reason may be the feeling that it would create extra work
in remedial teaching. Terry notes that girls are already disadvantaged in Year 7 woodwork, which is compulsory for all at
Rockwell High. The teaching is supposed to presuppose nothing,
but in practice assumes some familiarity with tools. Most of the
boys have learnt this from their fathers already, and very few of
the girls have. Another reason may be that the teachers know the
kids' and parents' choices are constantly made in relation to a
massively segregated labour market, something the school can do
little about.

Terry is very conscious of the parents as a presence in the
school. He sees their pressure as mainly conservative.

> We are obeying tradition more through the public, the people we
> serve, than through the staff.

He feels that parents have a right to access, to influence in the
school, and that there are now too many bureaucratic barriers
between parents and teachers. There is a breakdown in communication; one reason, he feels, for parents not having a high
regard for what the school does. He would like to do his bit to
communicate more, but does not have the time. As things stand,
given the demands on him, the best he can do is concentrate his
time and energy on the kids. To have a very different relation
with the parents would require a major reconstruction of his job.
He does not have the power to bring that about.

If he had, he might be able to clear up what he sees as a
major misunderstanding of his own subject. Parents and students
think it is about training for adult jobs. Terry knows his department does not have the equipment needed for that, for instance
up-to-date industrial lathes. In one of the bitterest moments in
the interview he says:

> The higher-ups tried to give us the impression we're educating for
> leisure not jobs. The kids look on it as a start for a job. With our
> toy lathes we couldn't presume to teach job skills. We can't
> educate them for a job. No way in the world.

So even in his own specialty he is letting the kids down. And the
official rationalisation of the situation, that they are 'educating

for leisure' and building skills for the home workshop, is little
comfort. It marginalises his subject even more.

The tangled and tense relationship between the working-class
school and its clientele is focused in Terry's life by the fact of
living in the neighbourhood. He feels he is part of the area, but
does not like it particularly, and would not recommend it. One
reason is that he copped some of the anger the school generates.
Boys from the school, not his own students but ones who had
some grievance with the institution, would get drunk and roll
around to his house after midnight. They would scream abuse
outside his door, throw rubbish into the yard, throw bricks and
bottles onto the roof. Terry notes philosophically

> They were trying to get at the school, not at me or people
> associated with me.

Even so, it could hardly be pleasant to be on the receiving end of
that raw hostility. We can understand that his view of the
school's clientele is not exactly rose-tinted.

Running the school

In new outer suburbs the schools are among the few large
institutions of any kind, sometimes the only public institutions
for miles. This is true in Rockwell, where the kids have to catch
a bus several miles to the nearest public swimming pool, and
their parents have to drive nearly as far to the nearest pub. The
high school capitalised on this (if that is quite the word) by
starting a weekly Bingo night. It is quite popular in the neighbourhood, and brings in several hundred dollars a week for the
school. The Bingo organisers claim credit for the school bus, two
colour video–recorders, four cameras, sundry other equipment,
and even much of the new school hall. Terry Petersen is one of
the three staff members who run it, and this is one of the things
that give him a solid place in the school's regime.

Terry's place is guaranteed by two other facts. As already
mentioned, he is one of the longest-serving members of staff. He
came to Rockwell High when it had only three forms and thirty
staff; he has seen it grow and change. He regrets the loss of the
old intimacy, where everyone knew everyone: 'the better you get
to know the staff, the better you get to know the kids'. The
teachers are now dispersed among different staffrooms and

people do not mix so much. He has seen changes in intake, changes in curriculum, and heavy turnover of staff; he has watched bosses and deputies, enthusiasts and radicals, come and go. Terry is a stayer, a survivor. That alone makes him an influence on the way the school works.

Finally, he is senior teacher in his own subject area and hence, however low the prestige of manual arts, part of the school 'executive'. He does not like administration much, but takes this part of his job seriously, especially the relationship with younger teachers on his staff:

> You're involved in a bit of philosophy, and a bit of grass roots
> stuff, you know. And not dictating, but trying to guide the
> thoughts of the staff, unless they believe it's hopeless.

He is pleased that a recent development, film screenings in the new hall, has released staff for proper departmental meetings. Questions of curriculum, assessment and reporting can now be thrashed out in general discussion, rather than being decided by the head of department.

But that is not the way things run in the school as a whole. Terry is always reluctant to criticise his colleagues, but makes it clear that in his view the present principal is boss and likes to keep it that way. On questions of the allocation of money there is no discussion beyond the executive, and no real negotiation; the principal decides. On other issues the teaching staff in general meet, but not very fruitfully. Terry comments on a general meeting of staff that was supposed to decide on a discipline policy:

> We go from three-fifteen to four o'clock, three-quarters of an
> hour. I don't know how General Motors would go, running their
> show in three-quarters of an hour. There's not time, in the way
> the schools have been organised, for the school staff to get
> together and effectively discuss the important issues that make a
> school function.

Another problem with 'democracy' is that some deep divisions have opened up among the staff. The separation between departments Terry noted as a trend in the history of the school has now become the basis for what he sees as an unhealthy degree of factionalism. There is conflict over funding to the various subject areas. More seriously, there is a good deal of antipathy

over approaches to teaching, some departments taking a progressive line and others a traditional one. Everybody knows
about this, but it is not brought into the open. The principal
tries to act as mediator, and to include both approaches. It is not
an easy row to hoe.

So Rockwell High is far from a smoothly-functioning machine.
It is kept on the road, and in some kind of order, only by constant effort, an endless round of picking up the pieces, patching
up the machinery. A good deal of Terry's work as head of
department is doing that kind of job. The resources are not there
to do it really well. The patching is often rough, and people get
knocked about in the process. Terry Petersen has come through
some rough patches himself. He has survived; like the school, he
keeps on going. So what, after a decade and a half at it, does he
make of being an educator?

Education

The first thing is that he plays down any notion of a 'calling'.

I look on teaching as my bread and butter. It's not a ministry.

Terry insists on clearly defined hours and routines, and resists
disruption to them. He is prepared to go the extra mile, as
witness his involvement in the Bingo enterprise; but only by his
own choice, and when he has worked out all the implications.

He is, in short, cautious. He has reason to be. The first and
last rule for someone spending their life in teaching is to survive
as a teacher. The pressures are sometimes fierce, and Terry has
had his share of battery to the ego: extreme isolation in his first
schools, the disrespect of other teachers for his subject, the
attacks of neighbourhood youth, and some other experiences
more personal and equally stressful. To treat teaching first and
foremost as a job is his way of drawing boundaries, placing
limits on the pressure that school life can place on him.

That is a reasonably common reaction among experienced
teachers. It easily appears to working-class parents, who know
very little about teaching as a job, as evidence that the teachers
'don't care' about their kids. This is one of their most common
criticisms of the school. So it is worth insisting that Terry *is*
interested in the kids he teaches. He takes trouble with them,
and basically likes his work. Treating it as a job rather than a

'ministry' is not just a defensive reaction. It is an approach that gives shape to a whole perspective on education.

It is, for instance, closely connected to his positive regard for his fellow workers. It is characteristic that even in a confidential interview Terry was very reluctant to make criticisms of other teachers on the staff, except in the most indirect ways. He takes trouble over the induction of new staff. He is worried about economic trends in the industry, notably increased teaching loads and class sizes, frozen promotion, and teacher unemployment. He is scathing about the Department's failure to offer jobs to new teachers who have just completed teacher training courses. His industrial position is hardening.

All this is tied together by identification with teachers as a group, as a kind of occupational community. He never comes out with grand philosophical propositions about the cultural role of education. But it is plain that he regards teaching as a useful and difficult thing to do, a job that has some dignity. There are overtones of the old-fashioned tradesman in this, a dash of craft unionism, as well as up-to-date professionalism.

Another aspect of treating teaching as a job is that it encourages him to be coolly realistic about its circumstances and impact. Terry knows very well what he can and cannot achieve in this milieu. He knows things about labour markets and job prospects that teachers like Sheila Goffman and Margaret Blackall do not. Because the fate of kids at schools like this is basically a collective fate, he can, in principle, be much more of a resource for the majority of them.

Terry classifies the manual arts department among the 'conservatives' in the school, and that certainly is the flavour of his own approach to education. Broadly speaking he feels that teachers hold the knowledge which working–class kids and their parents need but do not have. Those who don't should take direction from those who do have it. This is not so much an explicit argument as a commonsense assumption that to get on, you need to do well at school; conventionally defined school knowledge is therefore unproblematically appropriate. The reason most working-class kids do not 'get on' is that they have not latched on to this truth. The system lets them drift through. Terry would like to see them working hard, and actually earning their School Certificate.

In many ways Terry's outlook is like prevailing views among

the parents. He is the kind of teacher who might construct a very positive relation between the working class and education. The circumstances of his life and the exigencies of the school prevent this. Paradoxically it is Sheila Goffman, much more remote from the local milieu, who has more sense of the possibilities. But her practice only works with a minority. Terry is working with the majority, and that is where the crucial questions lie.

3

Angus Barr

The elite private schools are very different institutions from working-class comprehensives like Greenway and Rockwell High. Wellington College, an old-established private school with a clientele of graziers, farmers, city businessmen and affluent professionals, is definitely part of the establishment. Angus Barr is one of the 'key men' (his own phrase, and perfectly justified) in it. Rising 50 at the time we interviewed him, he is, like Terry Petersen, the senior teacher in his subject area; in Wellington phraseology, The Language Master. He is articulate, at times eloquent; very well informed about everything to do with the school and its environment; confident of his own judgments, though not dogmatic; an active participant in professional organisations; a man who takes responsibility and makes things happen. He is one of the people who really make the private school system tick.

The teaching career

Angus went to school at a famous grammar school in another city. We know nothing of his family except for an indication that he was the first generation to go to such a school, so it may have been on a scholarship. He did well, went on to university, and came out several years later with an Arts degree.

Uncertain of his future, he decided to travel and look around, keeping body and soul together by picking up teaching jobs in private schools which at the time were glad to have a fully-fledged graduate. On one of these jobs he met a girl from a neighbouring private school, married, and found himself settled. Thirteen years later he was still settled, and beginning to feel too much so.

I could have stayed on at St Andrew's till I was 65. I had a
boarding house, and lived in, and everything else. And I was
settled and insulated and insular. And I got to the stage where I
got sick of doing the same thing over again. I thought 'I've got to
go till I'm 65' and it would drive me up the wall. And I found I
was getting cranky with boys. They were no longer amusing me,
and I think I was becoming a bit blasé, cynical, sour and vinegary.
And a schoolmaster has got to watch this, it's a great danger.

So I came over here, and Napier [the Headmaster at Wellington
College] said 'I've got something going here if you're interested'.
And seeing as he offered me more money—not that that was any
inducement (laugh)—so I came. And I would think that one of the
good aspects of the state system is that it does provide for
mobility. And I think that from a personal point of view, and
from an experience and professional point of view that it's good.

What Mr Napier offered was, in fact, the chance to become
subject senior not very much later. Angus Barr seized the chance
with both hands. He put his energy into renovating what had
become a run-down department. He extended his network of
contacts in the other private schools, to get new ideas and recruit
interesting staff. He became more active in the Modern
Languages Association, a representative on syllabus committees,
a well known figure in his field. He sits on Wellington College's
scholarship committee, maintains contacts with the boys'
families, and in various other ways is an influential presence in
the school.

In short, Angus has become more deeply involved in the world
of the private schools as he has risen within it. He is now near
the peak of his career, and with some urging from his wife is
contemplating applying for headmasterships. He has given some
thought to what he would do if he got a school of his own.

As a headmaster I think the things I'd be principally concerned
with would be efficient organisation and administration, an
emphasis on scholastic standards, and the development of goodwill,
you know, friendly pleasant relations with boys and parents. I
think first of all a headmaster has got to administer and organise
well, otherwise he's not successful. I'm concerned with academic
standards very much. I'm not a games-above-everything-else person
at all; I keep them in their right place. I wouldn't be a great
innovator, I don't think, from any preconceived ideas. When I saw
a situation in which there became the need for innovation, I would
innovate. But I haven't any real preconceptions about things I

desperately urgently believe had to be done and my destiny to do,
some burning passion to make the study of Indonesian universal
and that sort of thing.

So Angus sees himself as a conserver of traditions. But he also
sees himself as a professional, and has a well-articulated view
that teaching should be seen as a profession. He waxes bitter
about its lack of public recognition—'I think teaching is still a
most despised and rejected profession'—and blames 'irrespon-
sible' teachers in the private schools, as well as the activities of
the state teachers' union, for this.

What is interesting about Angus Barr's strong endorsement of
professionalism is that it has few connotations of special
expertise. Granted, teachers and schools have to know their
business to be able to satisfy the clients; but that business is not,
after all, a very arcane one. Angus, along with many other staff
recruited by Mr Napier, had no teacher training. It is ethos
rather than technique that weighs most heavily with the headmaster. As his sketch of himself as headmaster implies, Angus
has no drive towards innovation, no programme he urgently
wants to implement. His concern is managing things, keeping
things going.

And that is consistent with his view of the immediate milieu.
For he excepts Wellington College's clientele from the general
charge of the public's disrespect for teachers. Wellington's
'community', as he calls it, does have a high regard for teachers,
and the main reason for this is long-serving teachers who have
stuck with the school for 30 or 40 years. Standards are set and,
it appears, policed:

Sometimes you can get a man coming along and saying to you,
'Well, I was terribly disappointed to see Mr So-and-so do this, or
not do that', on a particular occasion. It doesn't seem in
accordance with the traditions or practices of Wellington masters—
and I think they're the reflection of this school.

What professionalism means to Angus is above all a claim to a
definite status, a parity of esteem with the acknowledged professionals in the school's clientele. This esteem has to be earned,
and loyalty and regularity of conduct are the coin in which one
pays. Hence his annoyance at noisy unionism and scruffy
radicals, and his acquiescence in Wellington College's well-
established practice of quietly removing dissidents from the staff.

The space that technical expertise occupies in other views of the profession is filled, in Angus's practice, by an unusually active construction of relations among teachers in different schools. People moving from one job to another, like his own move from St Andrew's to Wellington, bring a skein of contacts with them. He is active in his subject association, and in syllabus committees. He arranges dances, in cooperation with the staff of a girls' private school; goes to functions that bring together staff from the boys' private schools; and most often, because it is a weekly event, meets the staff of the schools that Wellington's cricket and football teams are playing. Further, he meets the staff of at least one other private school as a parent.

Though state school teachers are involved in some of this, the main focus is on other elite private schools. Angus's description of his own practices points us to the important fact of a teacher network operating through and linking up these schools. Angus reckons that he would know quite well half-a-dozen people in each of the major private schools in the city. Through this extensive system of contacts he learns about their people, policies and problems. He keeps this information up to date, and is readily able to give detailed and subtle accounts of the similarities and differences among those schools. This enables him, in fact virtually requires him, to think about issues from the perspective of the private school system rather than the parochial interests of a single school.

The practice of teaching

As a classroom teacher, Angus first describes himself as a traditionalist, strong on talk-and-chalk, 'very nearly a lecture style'. Unlike many subject seniors he makes a point of taking some of the *lowest* stream classes. There is an element of self-satire, but also pride in his ability to bring it off, in his vivid descriptions of classroom life:

> I'm very old-fashioned in education, anything that's happened since 1850 I'm very dubious about. The drilling... I find these boys something that gives them a great deal of security, and it gives them a sense of achievement. If you can get them to have some sort of sense of achievement, their faces light up and it's magnificent to see, you're warmed too. So if you've got a disciplined approach and a structured approach, you provide them

with that academic security that normally they wouldn't have.
You've got to declare your parameters very carefully.

and his remedial method with the slower kids:

Restricting the quantity, drilling, constant testing, teach a little, test
a little; in other words intensive. Marking every page, marking
every error out and ensuring he writes them in a book and that he
knows them, if he doesn't know them then he writes them out 50
times; this sort of thing. It probably sounds terribly Spartan. And
of course they take me on, you encourage that too. And I think
that if we'd had the open class set-up, there's no way...

He conscripts the parents, too:

My method of communicating with parents is to send them home
either good or bad work with a comment on it and ask for
parent's signature, and I keep them in touch with a full description
of how his work's going.

Not that they all respond, or that he would welcome too close
supervision. 'No news is good news' he remarks, well aware that
private school parents are not slow to speak if they are
dissatisfied. They are paying, after all.

But Angus's classes are not just rote-learning and nothing else.
He tries to build in an element of project work and activity
learning, even for the slow ones. In fact he recalls that he was
one of the people who successfully campaigned on syllabus and
exam committees, years before, to get rid of the highly formal
approach that had previously dominated language teaching. He
tries to make the subject a vehicle for learning about culture
more generally, and sets up debates and excursions for the senior
students especially.

Gives me a feeling of satisfaction and achievement in doing it, and
the boys seem to appreciate it. They come back to me and say 'we
appreciate how you taught us and the way you taught it Sir', and
many of them say it's a very good training for university work as
well. Which I think is probably right.

In short, Angus as a teacher is authoritative where it counts, but
allows a controlled exploration of alternatives.

This seems to be of a piece with his style as head of department. He is happy to see the youngsters, fresh from their Dip Ed
courses, put their energy into audio-visual methods.

The school is prepared to provide the equipment, and I will be interested to see how they get on.

He does not oppose, but he also does not give any lead in that direction. He is prepared to live and let live.

One reason why Angus can adopt a rather more laisser-faire approach to his department than Terry Petersen can is that he has much more say in its selection. Basically, a subject area in a Departmental state school gets the teachers the Department sends it. Angus, to a large extent, recruits his own. He uses his extensive network of contacts to find likely prospects,

someone whom I know of, whom I've met from other schools, or who I've taught here.

It is the headmaster who does the formal interviewing and makes the appointment, but it would be extremely unlikely for someone to be appointed in his subject area whom Angus had not vetted and approved.

He takes responsibility for their induction, once they arrive; but after that they have to prove themselves, produce their own initiatives. There does not seem to be the kind of collective process over which Terry Petersen is now presiding in manual arts at Rockwell High, nor a very active discussion of curriculum issues generally within this school.

One of the most interesting aspects of Angus's work as a teacher is his intervention in the kids' social life. Parents expect private schools to exercise a more complete control over the pupils than state schools can. This does not always please the kids, who find themselves burdened with rules, uniforms and other restrictions, and subjected to a degree of surveillance, that most of their age-mates escape. But the notion of 'pastoral care' or 'individual attention' is an important selling point for the private schools. They handle it in various ways. Perhaps the most common is the 'House' system, where a group of pupils is assigned a common identity and a common set of teachers as counsellors and friends, both of which they keep throughout their stay in the school. This is most real and practical when it is a question of a boarding house. Angus was a boarding house master for a good many years, and has vivid recollections of what it meant:

You run a boarding house where you've got them for 24 hours a day; ad you have some of those horrendous interviews that Mum and Dad want to yell at one another, and you in the middle. Or of children abandoned, and I've had that. I've seen children left in these schools for the whole of the six weeks holiday. I saw a very clear case I'll never forget, where everybody in the school went home for Easter except one, and he went home and his father sent him back. He said 'No, stay there, I'm remarried'. So I rang the father up and told him I thought the age of Dickens had passed, but apparently it hadn't. Anyway he took him in, but said as soon as we could get him back...

It is a useful reminder that ruling-class families do not always function smoothly either; and that ruling-class schools sometimes have to perform a welfare function as well as an organising and educating one.

This kind of responsibility continues. Learning about a case of group bullying in Year 9 that had developed outside the classroom, Angus leaned, discreetly but firmly, on the boys who were doing it, and it stopped. Deciding that the boys needed suitable contact with the opposite sex, he approached the teachers of an eligible girls' private school and organised joint dances. He is, of course, coach of various sporting teams and attends all their matches.

What Angus is doing in much of this is supervising the construction of a particular kind of masculinity among his charges; and he does it mainly by embodying a definite kind of authority. The connection of masculinity and authority is one of the main axes of our culture, and even where it is under challenge (as in Margaret Blackall's life) it is very resistant to change. In Angus Barr's life it is unproblematic and unchallenged. Women enter his professional world only at the margins. He always refers to the teachers at Wellington College as 'men', even though there are some women teachers on the staff. And the one moment in the interview when he comes out with sharp criticism of private schools, it is directed at married women teachers, precisely those who have rejected the convention that marriage means subordination to a husband's career:

I think the girls' Independent schools are finished because they've got a staff of almost entirely married women, who are more interested in buying the chops for tonight's dinner than teaching. I think the old fashioned spinster schoolmistress may be [history], but she's played a very important part in girls' schools. When you look at the list of staff of these girls' schools now, and see these married women, the first thing they're concerned about is picking their children up after school and then going out to buy the meat for tonight's dinner.

Married women, in short, cannot be proper professionals. This is uncharacteristically intolerant—Angus's style most of the time is studied in its liberalism—which is perhaps an indication of how deeply the issue is felt. As it happens, Angus is missing some important changes that *are* going on in the professional ethos of girls' private schools, and will be discussed shortly.

The elite private school

Angus has a good many opportunities for meeting the parents of the boys he teaches, and makes it his business to use them.

> It could happen in a number of ways. Firstly, if a boy does badly, not only academically but often in discipline, I would ask the parents to come and see me... But it can also happen at a school like this, there are a lot of families who you get to know because they come about the place a great deal, and you probably get to know them before the boy even comes into your form. Through contact in the cricket or football seasons; parents come to watch matches and you see them in that sort of way. In some cases parents contact us, and ask me about what their sons are doing... I would say that I know the parents of half the boys in my form each year, probably about half.

There are also school-based social events, his own rôle as a parent, his own social life. The elite private school is surrounded by a dense social network, and a teacher like Angus Barr is an active participant in it.

In consequence he has a detailed knowledge of a good section of the local ruling class. He notes that one boy in our sample comes from a family that produced a conservative premier; that another comes from a family with a 'good strong tradition of good living and plenty of pleasure'; that a chairman of the school council was related to an incumbent conservative federal minister; and so on. He has a sense of turnover in the class, the rise of new families and new industries, and of the different schools' relations to that. He notes, for instance, that Wellington College draws from 'more securely established families' than many other private schools which rely more on 'the first generation of private school parents'.

Even to talk of a dense social network does not fully convey the intimacy of a situation where three and four generations of a family may follow in each other's tracks, and where schools and families are so involved with each other that disputes over schooling are literally family quarrels that can simmer for generations. Angus recounts a case in point:

> As you know there is a peculiar split in this family, where the father's brother sent his boys to Scotch, whereas this boy came here. But I think that was some personal row with Adamson [the previous headmaster at Wellington, now dead] at some time, which even old Bob Carnegie [the boys' grandfather] might have had. Adamson did have these rows which split families. There is another family, the Daveys, which is a strong Wellington family from the north-west, one of whose members had a huge row with Adamson, 30 years or more ago, based on his alleged rudeness. And their family went to Scotch as well.

Angus's active concern with this network does not imply subservience to it. I have already mentioned his tearing a strip off the father who returned his son to boarding school at Easter. Another instance is his view of Mr Wilson, the father of one of his present charges:

> His father strikes me as I would have expected: very strong character and quite certain he knows all the answers. He tells the boy at some times such extraordinary things that one would think that he believes that a lot of the things the school does are crazy and stupid.

He blames the father's influence for much of this boy's pigheadedness and unwillingness to take advice.

As this suggests, Angus has a clear sense of the proper relationship between parents and the school. The parents are, indeed, the clients and have a kind of ultimate say. The school will fold without their support. It wants their active involvement too, at functions, at sports, in fund-raising, and so on. But they should not interfere within the teachers' professional demesne.

> I think the parents' right is to choose the school which they are going to send their child. And if they make the choice knowing the nature of the school and knowing its traditions and organisation and administration, and they send the child to the school accepting the nature of the school, that therefore denies them any right to interfere in the administration of the school. If they don't like the school, they can take their son away. You know, how much is it

that the shareholders of BHP have a direct part in the
administration of BHP?

No doubt the analogy goes down well in the stockbroker belt.
We have, indeed, heard almost the same words from some
Wellington College parents. It defines a relationship that, when
working well, gives the school both the support and the space it
needs, not only to meet current demand but also to act strate-
gically, take the long view, modernise its practices, and in so
doing reconstitute the class it serves.

To do that, the elite private school cannot function mechan-
ically. It must grapple with dilemmas of policy and strategy. One
is its relation to the gender system. Some private schools have
gone coeducational; Wellington has not. Another is to decide the
stress to be laid on academic achievement and selection for
ability. During the last generation the intensity of academic competition at matriculation has increased markedly, and the private
schools have been struggling to keep their historic dominance.
Angus notes that the sons of old boys tend to be the 'dull ones',
liberally scattered through the C stream; it is the bright sons of
new families who provide the academic sparkle at Wellington
College. Should the school select at entry mainly for talent, thus
increasing the chances of gaining academic prestige at matriculation level? Or should it give more weight to the family
connections that have sustained it in the past, and may be
needed again?

It is people like Angus Barr who have to work out solutions to
such problems, and then make the solutions work. He has mixed
feelings about the issue of coeducation; in the end he settles for
a market solution, suggesting there are virtues in having some of
each so parents can pick what they want. Though there is an
element of market segmentation in his thinking about the second
question too, that cannot be handled in the same way as it is
already an issue internal to the school. Angus has no clear-cut
answer to it. As his remarks on being a headmaster indicate, it is
something he would hope to handle as a question of balance
among the different concerns of the school.

If the relationship works well, such teachers and their schools
perform a vital role for their clientele considered as a whole
social class. But the relationship does not always work well.
Wellington College, though its waiting lists are full and its
accounts buoyant, has its troubles. The contretemps between

Angus Barr and Mr Wilson is significant. For despite Angus's
account of it we know, having interviewed Mr Wilson too, that
this father does have reasoned criticisms of the school. He is a
technocrat, a high-powered and successful professional, who
wants his son to follow the same path. From his point of view a
lot of the attitudes he encounters at the school are archaic.
Angus Barr's stately minuet of balances, boundaries, and mutual
respect is more than a trifle old-hat. The real world of corporate
capitalism is a very different proposition.

Indeed there is a sense in which Angus's view of the world is a
cloistered one. His life has been mostly spent inside the private
school system, and he has never had to struggle to get where he
is. No wonder he looks a little askance at brash parents, at the
antics of teacher unions, at the dark and dangerous world
beyond the elite private schools. It would be unfair to suggest he
is simply complacent. He is alert, sharp as a tack about things
within his bailiwick, and probably the most liberal-minded
member of the senior staff at Wellington. But one still has a
strong feeling that this is a place where the recession has not yet
come.

4

Rosa Marshall

Rosa Marshall is one of the new breed of 'spinster schoolmis-tresses' who, with the aid of those married women against whom Angus Barr inveighs, are transforming the girls' private school scene. She is in her mid thirties, and a mathematics teacher at St Margaret's College, an institution for young ladies that caters to a clientele reasonably similar to Wellington's. She is also a socialist, a feminist, and a totally dedicated professional teacher. The combination is electrifying.

To the private sector

Rosa comes from a working-class background as solid as Terry Petersen's. She grew up in an industrial town; her father is a metalworker, and her mother worked in a shop during Rosa's childhood. The family was close, and both parents gave the children strong encouragement to do well at school and get on in the world. Much of Rosa's personal confidence, intellectual interest and political outlook grow from these roots. Her father, a thoughtful and well-read man, is an active unionist, and her mother a strong believer in the need for women to have their own careers. Neither had any secondary education, but were all the more determined that their children would get full measure.

With this support Rosa did well at the local high school, matriculated, and went to university to do a BA and DipEd. She had wanted to be a teacher as far back as she can remember. It is a familiar choice for someone moving along her path, and one that her family endorsed. The only unusual thing about it was her commitment to the most hard-edged of academic teaching subjects, mathematics, which is still not a common choice for girls. The state Department of Education accepted her out of the DipEd and packed her off to the country.

The next few years were the worst of her life. She was sent hither and yon, to four schools in five years. She faced the same problems of control as Sheila Goffman and Margaret Blackall, and wondered whether she was even doing the job she was trained for:

> Quite often the behaviour of the students was such that you weren't teaching your subject at all. You were in a sense correcting behaviour all the time, trying to mould them into some sort of social being rather than teaching a subject. And I always worried about moulding them into social beings, because I don't regard myself (laughing) as some kind of judge. And I'm not sure about what I think is the right sort of product that the school should turn out anyway.

But there was no doubt about the strain it was putting on her. She took a couple of years off to go overseas and broaden her experience. When she got back, the crunch came. She was posted to a school at the other end of the city, involving hours of travel.

> When I got there, as is usual in a state school, when you're new on staff you get all bottom classes...I was expected to teach not only maths and science, but had to teach sex education to a group of Year 7 kids. I found myself a bit horrified that they knew so much and had such ghastly attitudes. They ridiculed the whole thing and made it just sort of some animal function. They had no idea of—no one had ever talked to them about emotions, sex had been taught in a kind of factual vacuum. They hadn't seen there was love in there somewhere.

Things were little better when she was teaching senior classes:

> There were a number of migrants who spoke no English. Nothing was done. The subject senior sort of saw that as being normal. The kids sit doing nothing and gradually pick up the language. I went to the headmaster. He likewise thought I was a bit strange.

In the bottom-stream classes she was assigned, the curriculum itself proved a barrier to teaching:

> I really need the kids to like me in order to give them what I have to give. This means selecting the material they study very carefully, so they get some enjoyment out of it.

But she was not allowed to do this. The syllabus was laid down, the text books were set (in truth the school probably had little choice), and Rosa was obliged to teach from them.

Faced with massive resistance, given little support from the hierarchy, physically tired from the travel, totally frustrated professionally, Rosa Marshall quit—and the state system lost a dedicated teacher. She had answered a job advertisement at St Margaret's, and has never regretted it.

In the private school

St Margaret's is one of a number of girls' private schools currently undergoing something of an academic renovation. Under the previous headmistress (who appointed Rosa) the school, without actually losing its clientele or reputation, had by general repute become a bit slack. Staff morale was not good, decision-making was centralised but slow, parents were grumbling. Under a new principal there has been a marked tightening of standards. Administration has become brisk, parents and teachers get their answers promptly. There have been blitzes on the girls' uniform, punctuality, and conduct. Above all there has been a new emphasis on academic performance, a beefing–up of the school's commitment to high Matriculation results, and especially a new stress on maths and sciences.

Rosa Marshall has been caught up in this from the start—in fact she was doing it before the new headmistress arrived. It was not just a matter of her own subject. She was interested in new teaching methods, and became very involved in setting up an audio–visual resources centre in the school, training other teachers in its use, and integrating it into the overall curriculum. Indeed she could have become an audio-visual specialist, but held back:

> I either had to get more involved with the A–V scene, which I was
> quite interested in but the technical side of it left me cold. You
> had to go into that and really understand it. And my most useful
> talents were sitting in the classroom, where nobody could get at you.

She knew she was a good teacher, and stayed with her classes.

The change of regime has given her enormous scope on this side too. She thinks that St Margaret's will become 'a first–class mathematical school', and is doing everything she can to make sure it does. As a teacher she is didactic, uncompromising about the subject matter, but also focuses closely on the learner. Being in a classroom with her is a pretty intense experience.

For a large proportion of her students, it works. Rosa has a knack of getting them to do things her way, and then turning back on that and bit by bit showing them they can do it their way. She is also skilful at coping with the underlying lack of confidence with which most girls approach maths. She sees this as an emotional problem; as she puts it, the maths teacher cannot be a technician. Potential high flyers she encourages, stimulates, pushes hard, and in turn is stretched by them.

The energy she puts into teaching, and the satisfaction she gets out of it, build on each other. She puts in long hours. Most teachers at St Margaret's think they work longer than teachers in state schools, though they have fewer timetabled face-to-face hours and smaller classes. The kids themselves keep up the pressure, demanding rapid feedback on their written work, queuing outside the staffroom to get help, and so forth. Rosa is at school from 8.30 to at least 3.30 every day, prepares and marks for another hour each night and a couple of hours on Sundays. Besides her regular teaching there are extra-curricular activities such as the debating club, after-hours coaching of the girls, curriculum development in her own department, in-service conferences, keeping contact with the parents, looking to the 'pastoral care' of the girls, and sundry other tasks. St Margaret's does not go in for 'houses' in the way Angus Barr's schools do, but assigns 'form teachers' to keep contact with the girls across the range of their school life. Rosa, predictably, is one. She also takes an active part in general policy debates around the school.

All this implies a particular kind of context. When the previous headmistress retired, the staff—Rosa among them—told the School Council that they wanted a more democratic management; and this has, at least formally, been granted. There is now a lot more delegation and much more open consultation and discussion. It is a moot point whether this has meant any real loss of power for the principal, but it means a stronger sense among the teachers that the school works by consensus, that they are all in it together, that the school is their project. And it certainly means that classroom teachers get what for many of them counts most: responsibility for what they are doing in class, and room to develop their own practice.

But the cosiness of this picture should not be exaggerated. The new consensus does not embrace all the staff. Older teachers settled in their ways, and others who oppose the new policies, can be pretty uncomfortable. Building up the new regime has also required some fairly heavy pressure on the pupils. Rosa Marshall the factory-town girl finds much of this distasteful: the ludicrous uniform, rigidly enforced; the la-de-dah manners and silly school rules, such as always wearing hats in the street and not eating in public; the general atmosphere of conservatism and conformity. She thinks the school is too much concerned with its image. Sometimes the girls themselves bite back; they are not under total control.

Nor has St Margaret's solved all its policy problems. There is a long-standing debate in the school about streaming, and there have been some experiments, not decisive, with unstreamed subjects. In recent years this has taken a new shape, a debate over alternative non-academic curricula for students who are not headed for university. The problem is a difficult one for St Margaret's, and the staff are split. The school's internal renovation has gone together with a marketing strategy of stressing its academic results and its ability to get girls into higher education. This has its risks in the market: the narrower the offerings, the narrower the potential custom. St Margaret's is in competition with other girls' colleges, it has its financial problems, and it needs to keep its books full. Finally there is the matter of christian philosophy. The school is a church foundation, and some argue that as a christian institution it should be open to all.

Rosa Marshall can see through that one. She is well aware that the main requirement for coming to a school like St Margaret's is money. And she is by no means insensitive to the plight of the non–academics. She knows that 'a large group of girls go through here failing' because of the way the curriculum is geared. But she still firmly endorses the 'elitist' side of the alternative curriculum debate, thinking that the school should go on doing what it now does best. Her endorsement carries extra weight because she is known in the school as a radical.

I think a major reason she takes that position is the importance of the academic curriculum in her own life. Not that she has to be defensive about her own skills; they will not go out of fashion. Rather, academic knowledge is central to her professionalism, to her notion of what teaching is about. More, academic knowledge has been central to her ability as a woman to construct a career. And it is the key to her hopes for enabling

many of her pupils to do the same in their lives. She has criticisms of the competitive academic curriculum, but she also, like
Margaret Blackall, has a tremendous investment in it.

The house radical

Rosa's critique of the conservatism of the school is part of a
broader social radicalism. From her parents she inherited an
interest in labour politics, and she has a considerable number of
friends and contacts in the unions. She went to university in a
vintage period of student activism, during the campaigns against
the Vietnam war, and went on the streets in that mobilisation.
She describes herself as a socialist, and is strongly at odds with
the conservative politics of most St Margaret's families.

Further, she describes herself as a feminist. This is a more
recent development, though she may well have been started in
this direction by her mother's example. Her awareness of sexism
has grown from her experience of men both at work and in
social life. When she began teaching in the state system she took
for granted things like the subject seniors all being men, the
authority of the headmaster. She does not accept them now. She
believes strongly in the importance of economic independence for
women, and in her own life has taken a deliberate decision not
to get married so as to stay independent and concentrate on her
career.

She has given a good deal of thought to questions of gender
and education, and her answers are by no means the conventional ones. Rather than fill the school with female 'role models'
like herself, she would like to see equal numbers of men and
women on the staff, equally spread across departments. This is
not a popular view with the mostly female staff. And she is
sharply critical of sex-segregated schooling. Acknowledging that
girls in coeducational schools are not encouraged as they should
be to do 'non-feminine' subjects like maths and science, she still
sees the girls in single-sex schools as being 'disadvantaged
socially'. She describes their immature behaviour—'crazy, acting
out, yahooing, whistling, giggling and carrying on'—in the
street, or when a group of men or boys come to the school. You
can get 'a kind of hysteria' welling up in an all-girls' school, too
much jealousy and envy. That is not what the emancipation of
women is about, for Rosa. So she thinks it is better to battle it

out in the co-ed situation, nearer to hard reality.

So why is she at St Margaret's? Rosa acknowledges the problem:

> I am a constant astonishment to myself and my friends. My politics and my ideals go one way, and then how I actually live my day-to-day life is something quite the opposite. They're two warring sides that I just accept as being part of me.

The short answer, and almost the whole answer, is that the job she holds is the answer to a professional teacher's prayer. After years of frustration and disappointment in the state system, she has landed in a post that challenges and rewards her as a teacher, gives scope for her imagination and outlets for her abounding energies. She is respected by her students and her colleagues, feels part of a collective enterprise, and has been able to integrate this with an independent personal life.

Of course she is conscious that she is working for the children of the rich. She is even aware that the conditions of her rewarding professional life are bound up with things about the school she dislikes, notably its conformism. The ethos here, among parents and in the school as a whole, channels the kids towards compliance with the teachers' project. The girls go along with what their parents want, which is usually to do well at school, get good reports, and if possible go to university. The few who do not conform can be got rid of.

Such a school is in danger from its own conservatism. This is the qualification to the suggestion that Rosa sticks it only because of the professional rewards. There is also a role for a radical here, as stirrer. Rosa sees herself in some measure as The Opposition, waging a battle against complacency and conservatism. Partly this is directed to the staff, who may be good teachers but most of whom come from the same milieu, many in fact being St Margaret's old girls. This is where she directs her arguments about uniform, rules, and the like.

More importantly it is directed to the girls. Most of them come from 'true blue' families and are anti-Labor, anti-union, and all the rest of it. Rosa and other teachers like her think it is very much the school's business to give the other side of things. For instance when a big industrial dispute is on, they make the girls discuss it calmly and from the union's point of view. A vignette: at a time when there was sharp political debate about stopping uranium mining, the chief executive from a big uranium mining company was invited to the school to address the senior girls. It was arranged through the headmistress, and in this case without consultation with the staff. Rosa and her mates were offended. 'Right, we're going to see both sides of this picture!' They got together and provided fact sheets for the girls, with arguments for and against, and sample questions. When the mining magnate turned up, the girls roasted him.

Here Rosa's politics connect up with traditional educational ideology, valuing open, balanced, rational discussion. But apart from issues like uranium, where there is already dissent among the affluent, she is swimming against the tide. Even if she succeeds in making the girls more open-minded, she is in effect giving new skills and new capacities for successful management to the already privileged. She remains uneasy about the situation, unable to reconcile her 'two warring sides'. But so much is happening in her teaching life, so much that is good, that she does not stay awake at nights agonising about it.

From her clients' point of view, Rosa is an exceptionally good buy. They may not like her politics much; there have been one or two delicate moments with parents. But for their money they are getting enthusiasm and imagination, total commitment to the project of teaching, formidable technical skill, and what seems to be inexhaustible energy. The school's achievement in harnessing the talents and energies of teachers like Rosa is impressive. It is one of the real success stories of the current educational scene. Conversely, it is teachers like this who make such schools hum. Institutions do not function by themselves; they have to be made to work, and with schools it is mainly the teachers who are doing it. Rosa Marshall's professional pride is justified. Perhaps her political unease is too.

5

Jack Ryan

The five teachers introduced so far all work in the mainstream. They teach conventionally-defined subjects to conventionally-organised classes; their working lives are basically organised by the logic of the academic curriculum, even Terry Petersen's. Yet that curriculum itself is the source of many of the difficulties they face, and particularly of the resistance encountered at schools like Greenway and Rockwell High. Jack Ryan is a teacher who is doing something rare and difficult—getting the resisters at a working–class comprehensive to shape up and learn —partly because he has moved outside its ambit. What he has done, and the circumstances that have enabled him to do it, are interesting and important.

Teaching for survival

Jack has an unusually clear and tough-minded view of the working-class school's task. He starts with blunt facts. The kids have to get jobs; most of the jobs they can get are not up to much; the school has to help them get the jobs. At the moment it does not. A major reason for this is the academic curriculum, which makes lots of kids flog away doing work they dislike and will never use. He is in favour of more usable, vocational material, especially in fields like Commerce and English.

But he is no simple pragmatist. The school also has a larger task, to

> turn out a person who will become a good citizen, who has
> developed his own self at the same time.

He wants a broad, engaging curriculum. He would like to see controversial issues taught, and is concerned about multi-cultural education.

The trouble with the current organisation of teaching is that it

actively *prevents* these things happening for large numbers of
kids. Margaret Blackall gave a vivid description of the moment
at which secondary streaming first hits the lower-stream children
(p. 17). Jack Ryan has an equally vivid, and much more extensive, knowledge of what happens to them thereafter.

This is not to say he rejects academic knowledge, or the
academic curriculum, or even streaming. He is an 'educational
conservative', in his own words. Like Terry Petersen he identifies
strongly with the occupational community of teachers, and that
almost inevitably involves some commitment to the academic
knowledge that is presently at the core of teachers' professional
self-definition. But he is more ambivalent about it than most
teachers. He can see there is damage being done.

One reason he can see this is that some of it was done to him.
He was teaching, or trying to teach, a mainstream subject in a
traditionally-organised high school; and had such a rough time
of it that, like Rosa Marshall, he very nearly quit. In fact Jack
would have left teaching altogether, if it had not been for a
young family and a mortgage. Instead he made two shifts that
began to change the terms of the problem for him. He moved to
a new school, and to a new framework of teaching. He is, and
has been for the last half-dozen years, Rockwell High's specialist
remedial teacher.

What this means, officially, is that he works with 'under-
achieving' pupils, outside their normal classes, individually or in
small groups, trying to develop their reading, writing, and arith-
metic. Some of that is very basic teaching indeed, as there are
Anglo teenagers at the school who are still virtually illiterate, and
migrants whose mastery of English is very shaky. It is slow
work, not only for being technically 'remedial'. The kids sent to
him include a high proportion of youngsters who are not learning because they are angry with the school, resentful of the way
the education system has treated them, and hostile towards
teachers. He has to establish a different kind of relation with
them before he can even begin to teach. His attempts to do this
have led him a long way beyond the official definition of remedial teaching tasks. It is that wider practice that is the most
notable thing about his work.

The teacher and the working-class community

Concluding that one of the things the kids most desperately
needed was access to jobs, Jack set about getting it. He could

not do this from a classroom, nor from his office. He had to go out and look where the jobs were. Over the years he has built up an extensive network of contacts in local industry, and got wise in the ways of the labour market. The Ryan Labour Exchange, he laughingly calls it. In fact it is a real and important source of information for the kids at Rockwell High about what is on offer and how to get it.

Not just the conventional jobs either. Jack tells the story of one boy who was a disaster from the school's point of view: in the bottom stream, his father vanished, his mother in poverty, regarded as a hopeless learner, and never able to get to school before ten in the morning. Jack saw an advertisement for a job in a city record shop. He knew this boy could faultlessly reel off the Top 40 at the drop of a hat and knew an enormous amount about pop music, so he pointed him towards that job. The boy was hired, now rises regularly at six in the morning to get to work on time, and loves it.

In the immediate neighbourhood, Jack puts time and thought into cultivating the local employers. He visits and talks to them; he speaks to business organisations like Rotary and the Chamber of Commerce; he organises Work Experience programmes; he follows up the kids he has placed to see how they have gone. The result is that he has become not only a source of information, but a positive asset in getting jobs. His personal recommendation counts for more, around the traps, than the school's official assessments.

He also spends time getting to know the kids' families, by visiting the parents at home. This is so rare in the context of a school like Rockwell High that the parents are deeply impressed. Mr and Mrs Poulos, for instance, the parents of one of the school resisters in our sample, spoke warmly of Jack but of no other teacher. He visited them, and made comprehensible to them what was happening up at the school. He seemed to them to be 'taking trouble' with young Bill Poulos in a way no other teacher had.

> Mr Ryan gave him extra work, showed him extra things, all different mathematics and things. And whatever his weak subject was, he helped him along. I've got a lot of time for that Mr Ryan.
> *Did he have to work hard at home?*
> He worked no harder than the hours he worked after school with

Mr Ryan. He went to the park, he had his subject and his homework. And when he didn't know what to do he'd ask Mr Ryan, and he'd show him and tell. And he'd ask them first, he'd ask them some questions, to make them think. Like 'What is this?' and 'What happens when you do that?' to make them starting using their head a bit. This is the most important thing, to start making the students use their brains.

On his side, Jack Ryan came away knowing things about Bill which no other teacher at Rockwell High knew: for instance about the level of violence in his family background.

As a card-carrying realist Jack refuses to romanticise the families he deals with. Violence, prison terms, abandonment, poverty and chronic anxiety are all parts of the scene. (Rockwell High does not have an especially poor or socially disorganised clientele; this is a mainstream working-class situation.) Nor does he stereotype or patronise them. The 'single-parent family' is familiar in teachers' demonology as a source of trouble for the school. Jack does not assume that, saying of single parents he has met:

I think these people do a damn good job, accepting responsibility and bringing up the children, putting kids through school.

He will help, if there is trouble, but tries not to get in the way.

What he does, basically, is take parents seriously. He is scathing about a previous principal of the school 'treating parents like cretins without rights'. There is no great theory here about Democratic Control, Community Schooling, or whatever. It is simply good common sense, in Jack's view, to tie in what the school is doing with what the parents are doing, and to get some real flow of information and co-operation between them.

In the same low-key and undemonstrative way Jack establishes his relations with the kids themselves. His scheduled remedial classes are the starting point of his contacts with them, but not the end. He sometimes stays after school to coach them and help them with their homework for other classes. He sometimes drives them home. He sometimes hangs around for a game of billiards. He was the chief mover in the school's applying for a grant to get camping and bushwalking equipment; the grant came through, and that activity is now a regular part of the Rockwell school year.

In various ways, then, Jack has built up a large balance of credibility with the kids he is teaching. He is interested in them, and useful to them. He does not patronise them or have prejudices about them. He knows that most of them find school a place of anxiety mixed with boredom. He will work for them, but they have to put in effort too.

And a good many of them *do* respond, do 'try' for him in a way they will not for other teachers. His goal is to get them to learn enough 'basics' either to get back into the mainstream curriculum or to get a job. He tries to stop them fighting the school, since that gets them nowhere. He gives them reasons to regard the school as a resource rather than a kind of prison. Of course it does not work with all of them, as Jack freely admits. But given that he is dealing with the school's failures anyway, the successes have greater significance. And it is all a one-man operation: cheap at the price, for the school.

As far as we can tell, Jack's strategy is entirely home-grown. Some of it sounds like what a school-based social worker might do, but it is crucially different from that since it is based on teaching. What Jack has done is work out a way that a teacher, *as teacher*, can function as an organic part of a working-class neighbourhood, even one as dispersed and hegemonised as this outer suburb. That the approach has limits is obvious enough. What is remarkable is how far it has gone as an individual effort.

How he can do this

We know little about Jack's family background, except that he is probably no stranger to working-class life. He is a migrant, having come out from Britain as a young man, already trained as a teacher but not settled in a career. Rockwell High is only his second Australian school, and he has been here for half his career. He is married, has children and takes some part in Parents and Citizens activities in his kids' school.

Perhaps more important, he is a practising Roman Catholic, and of a particular kind, with a strong social conscience and no great love of the hierarchy. His religion is, we think, an important basis of his practice as a teacher. The kids who are shrugged off by some as 'the dodoes' are, for Jack, 'kids who need help'. He takes a basically moral view of the teacher's responsibilities.

Christian forbearance also seems to be an element of his insistence on not blaming the homes, or the kids, for being what they are. He will not entertain any notion of cultural or educational 'deficit'. But christian ethics may also inform his insistence that the kids have to take responsibility for what they now do.

Someone with this outlook could be a pain in the neck for his colleagues. Jack is not. He has made a shrewd assessment that he will get nowhere if the other staff are antagonistic to his work, and has set out to build bridges. He moves around the school a good deal, and is familiar with all its departments. He is a steady supporter of the teachers' union, and goes on strike when a strike is called. He takes the teachers' point of view, not the kids', on discipline issues: a significant point, given that he is teaching a lot of the resisters among the kids and needs their confidence too. He admires the 'iron-man' deputy head who always supports the staff, no matter what, in dust-ups with students or parents.

It is an essential condition of his work that the school hierarchy should support him. As his practice has developed, they have had increasing reason to. He is not only an effective remedial teacher but also a walking encyclopaedia of information about the district and its affairs. The present principal relies on him a great deal for background about the kids' families. Jack is no slouch where an opportunity for straight talking offers:

> He made the mistake of saying 'I like frankness', and he is obviously offended with some things I say. He'll say 'Gee, you must think I'm naive', and I say 'Yes'. 'Behind this desk I don't see any of that.'

Jack thus has a unique personal place in the school. He has a lot of autonomy, is subject to hardly any supervision or control. Not attached to any department—he has his own office, and floats around the various staffrooms—and with a direct line to the Boss, he does not have to take sides in the internal struggles for finance, or over school policy. He is conscious of the advantages for his relations with staff. On questions of pedagogy and curriculum he usually lines up with the conservatives, but manages not to antagonise the progressive departments. It is a delicate performance, brought off with patience and humour.

Jack's practice is also sustained by a distinctive outlook on the world. One aspect of this has already been mentioned, his almost militant realism. He calls the shots as he sees them, regardless of who is suited. He is no respecter of conventions or of authorities. Indeed there is a larrikin streak in him that comes out on such issues. A previous headmaster, whom Jack thought a bit of a stuffed shirt, had a private space painted for himself in the school parking lot; Jack promptly parked the Ryan-Mobile on it, and refused to move. Perhaps he needs the union!

He does, however, respect the ordinary people he deals with: the kids, their parents, other teachers. And he makes no distinctions in this respect. At this level he is a thorough-going egalitarian, though no political radical. He regards teachers as more knowledgeable than kids, and therefore properly in control of the learning process. He is utterly opposed to 'child-centred' pedagogy, and would never do the sort of thing Sheila Goffman (chapter 1) does. But he does not regard teachers as in any sense more enlightened people, or bearers of finer culture, or entitled to particular prestige. He is not the kind of conservative that Angus Barr (chapter 3) is.

An active and essential part of this outlook is that he rejects many of the stereotypes current in the education trade. He does not talk about 'low IQ', though that is the usual way of characterising the kids he deals with. He does not believe in the deleterious effects of working mothers, latch-key children, or broken homes. He does not believe any of the kids are unemployable, or incapable of learning, or no-hopers. He does not believe the schools have no connection with unemployment.

Finally, Jack's practice is sustained by a professionalism as real as Rosa Marshall's (chapter 4), if less flamboyant. He puts in as much time and energy as she does. Unlike Terry Petersen (chapter 2), he does think of teaching as a kind of ministry, a secular one to be sure. He is critical of teachers who do not put in a full day's effort, the 'nine-to-three-ers' as he calls them. And it is not any old day's work they are supposed to put in. Jack considers teaching is the kind of work in which one has to take responsibility for what one does. It is work that is really worth doing; as always, his views have a strong ethical component. It is also skilled work, often difficult to do. Jack is certainly tackling the most difficult end of it, getting the resisters to learn.

This adds up to an occupation that calls for all one's resources of imagination, skill, empathy and energy. What it does not add up to is any justification for elitism, prestige, or privileged treatment. Such a claim would, indeed, destroy Jack's own effectiveness in the situation he is facing.

Problems

Jack Ryan is a notable example of the inventiveness classroom teachers can show when facing problems that baffle the experts. He is doing one of the hardest jobs the whole education system has to offer. And in doing it he has worked out a practice with far-reaching implications for working-class schooling, notably in his construction of an organic relation between a state school and a working-class community.

At the same time we should note two strong limitations on Jack's effectiveness. One is the area of gender relations. His work is mainly with stroppy boys, who are the more conspicuous problem in his school. It probably does not work as well with stroppy girls. Jack's own brand of masculinity easily gets him on a wavelength with teenage boys, with interests like billiards, camping, and cars; but could equally be an obstacle to relations with teenage girls. He is familiar with the rough, male-dominated sexuality of the neighbourhood kids—the drunken weekend gang-bangs, the unpredicted but unprevented pregnancies (he reports that the girls won't take the pill because it makes them fat)—and is pretty uneasy with it. His practice does not give much grip on these issues.

Second, though he insists on facing uncomfortable facts, he rarely asks where the facts come from. Why is there this steady stream of 'kids who need help'? He does not like to call them 'working class', seeing that as another stereotype, and wants to deal with each one as an individual. So far as they have individual problems he does solve them, no one better. But many of the problems are in fact collective, such as the state of the education system and the state of the labour market.

Here Jack's unwillingness to think about the kids in terms of class relations is a serious drawback. It prevents him linking up with other people working on strategies for responding to those collective problems, such as youth workers and activists in the labour movement. Jack's self-conscious neutrality as a teacher holds him back from what he would see as partisanship. He does not blame the kids or the homes as deficient; that would contradict his christianity and his whole ethical outlook. He does not blame the education system; that is his life investment. These are strengths that make him effective at a grass-roots level. But there are problems that they do not give purchase on, and which must be addressed in other ways if Jack's individual practice is to become part of a larger strategy of reinvigorating working-class education.

Part Two
Teachers' Work

6

The labour process and division of labour

Teachers are workers, teaching is work, and the school is a workplace. These simple facts are often forgotten. Parents often judge teachers as if they were surrogate parents, kids treat them as a cross between a motorcycle cop and an encyclopaedia, politicians and media treat them as punching-bags. Nevertheless they are workers, and in understanding them it is essential to analyse their work.

Recent industrial sociology in studying other industries has emphasised three issues: the nature of the labour process, the division of labour, and the pattern of control and autonomy in the workplace. These are useful points of departure for the analysis of teachers' work; the first two are explored in this chapter, and control in chapter 9. They also lead to problems more specific to teaching, centred on the curriculum and the emotional texture of classroom interactions, which will be explored in chapters 7 and 8.

The task and its circumstances

Helping people to learn is a deceptively simple proposition. Phyllis Howell, Deputy Headmistress of St Margaret's College and a social science teacher of twenty years' experience, explains a basic point:

> You have to like kids, and be prepared to explain things over and over.

Len Johnson, English teacher at Greenway High School, a wry and thoughtful veteran of fifteen years in fairly tough state schools, suspects that however patient you are, teaching is somehow a mission impossible:

Provided that absolute chaos doesn't reign in the classroom, the
capable kid is going to acquire things just as he gets older. I mean,
in my subject English, it's *very* difficult to teach a kid English.
You can introduce him to different books—which I enjoy doing—
and authors, and so on; and you can read them and make them
exciting, and actually get them to do what they wouldn't have done
themselves. But as to improving their English: I don't think it can
be done, quite frankly.

Many teachers would agree. It is a cliché of the trade that you
cannot make someone learn, though you can help them if they
want to. Yet even that 'helping' is hard to specify. One gestures
with phrases like 'explaining things over and over', or 'getting
them to do what they wouldn't have done themselves'. Experienced and successful teachers like these often find it difficult to
say how it is done, or even what, precisely, they are doing.
Bettina Alt, a thoughtful and efficient mathematics teacher at
Auburn College, an elite girls' private school, reflects on the uses
of educational research like our project:

Very interesting. I don't know enough about what I'm doing. I
don't really know how to teach, except by the feel; because I don't
really know how people learn. I don't think anybody does. I think
what we're doing is very hit-and-miss.

There is something a little mysterious and evasive at the heart of
the business of teaching.

This can be put more formally. Teaching is a labour process
without an object. At best, it has an object so intangible—the
minds of the kids, or their capacity to learn—that it cannot be
specified in any but vague and metaphorical ways. A great deal
of work is done in schools, day in and day out, but this work
does not produce any *things*. Nor does it, like other white-collar
work, produce visible and quantifiable *effects*—so many pen-
sions paid, so many dollars turned over, so many patients cured.
The 'outcomes of teaching', to use the jargon of educational
research, are notoriously difficult to measure. There is even
room for debate whether the quality of teaching has any effect at
all; Len Johnson's opinion is not an isolated one.

I do not think it is right; and one reason is the view taken by
Len Johnson's own students, who do make clear distinctions
between good teaching and bad teaching, and much prefer the
good stuff. But the fact remains that it is always difficult to

specify the object of the teachers' labour, the raw material they are supposed to be working on. In consequence the definition of the task can expand and contract in quite alarming ways.

The popular image of schoolteaching is of talk-and-chalk in front of a class, and this still is a significant part of the day's work for many, perhaps most, teachers. Apart from principals, we only came across one teacher who never did any talk-and-chalk. But there is much more. Simply to list all the bits of work teachers mentioned to us in describing their relationships with kids would take pages.

Even talking at a blackboard implies time spent preparing the lesson, time spent getting the class settled and willing to listen, time spent supervising exercises and correcting them. Beyond this, running a class involves keeping order; dealing with conflicts between the kids; having a joke with them from time to time and building up some personal contact; discussing work with them individually; planning sequences of lessons; preparing handouts and physical materials; collecting, using and storing books and audiovisual aids; organising and marking tests and major exams; keeping records; liaison with other teachers in the same subject. Most of that has to be done separately for each class; and in the usual high school situation each teacher is dealing with a number of different classes each day.

That is for conventional classroom work. Beyond it there is a very wide range of jobs to be done to keep a school humming along, or even bumping along. Supervising the kids in play-grounds, at the canteen, at sporting events, onto transport, on excursions. Planning and arranging swimming carnivals, athletics days, football and netball matches, geography excursions, biology excursions and so on outside the school; drama work-shops, concerts, gymnastic displays, fetes, speech days, bingo nights and so forth inside it. Going to parent/teacher nights, Parents' and Citizens' Association meetings, union meetings, staff meetings, departmental meetings. Organising, getting facilities for, and supervising the school magazine, the chess club, the camera club, the debating teams, the students' council, the end-of-term disco, the farewell to Year 12. Making school rules, policing them, administering punishments. Being class patron (year teacher, form mistress, house master, etc), and coordinating information about members of the class, doing 'pastoral' work, checking rolls, answering queries. Counselling

kids in trouble, dealing with personal crises, with sexual and
ethnic antagonisms, with bullying; and sometimes dealing with
agitated parents, welfare officers, police. Modifying curricula,
bringing programmes up to date, integrating new materials;
getting familiar with new techniques, new machines, new textbooks; attending in-service conferences and courses on new
curricula. Planning and taking kids on camps, bushwalking,
canoeing, swimming. Writing end-of-term and end-of-year
reports, final references and other official documents.

This is far from being the full tally, but it is enough to
indicate the enormous range of tasks ordinarily done around a
school. There is no *logical* limit to the expansion of an individual
teacher's work into this yawning gulf. The more committed
teachers consequently work remarkably long hours—70 to 80
hours a week at peak times—though there is nothing obliging
them to do so. Others adopt the survival strategy that makes
them, in Jack Ryan's phrase, 'nine-to-three-ers'.

In another direction the lack of an object allows a limitless
intensification of teachers' work. 'We teach the individual',
Sheila Goffman proclaimed (chapter 1); but each individual
person is infinitely complex. Here is Mary Coleman, a young
teacher at Greenway High, sketching her relationship with Fay
McColl, a student she wants to push ahead:

Does she work well all the year?
Up and down—this is in English. In some subjects, in her language
subjects, she's been consistently good. In English, a lot of the time,
she didn't bother to pass up work, which brought her overall
assessment down. When she does her work it's usually at least a
B standard. I've written a few rude remarks on her English book,
through the year, to the effect that she should start working
instead of fiddling about. And for a while after that she's worked.
Then she'll slack off again, so she gets another little comment and
starts working again! I don't know whether it's just that she
doesn't like English, or whether she spends her time with other
subjects; and I think she's got a lot of interests outside school.
She's interested in horse-riding I think, and boys, and this film-
making thing.

The complexity of the relationship and its vicissitudes is obvious.
So is the further work Mary could immediately do: check with
the teachers in language about Fay's strategies there, find out
what Fay's real view of English is, re-organise her allocation of

individualism

time, try to build on her interests in horses and boys, expand the English curriculum to include films... And Mary, unlike her colleague Len Johnson, is convinced that her teaching effort counts. She remarks later in the interview:

If I really sit on a kid that's got writing problems, and if I really help them, and if I go over their work again and again, they do learn and they do improve.

The limit is not in that kid's capacity to absorb teaching, to use up Mary's labour-power; the teaching could become ever more intense. The limit is purely and simply the other demands on Mary's time and energy. She goes on:

But in the meantime, the rest of the class is playing up or doing something else while you're helping this one kid.

In practice, then, the labour-process-without-an-object is not an amorphous mess. It is very firmly shaped by circumstances and demands, both immediate and remote.

The physical and social space of the classroom is the most immediate of these pressures. A great deal of teaching is done with one adult and twenty or thirty kids in a fairly bare room together, with the door shut. This situation has a host of consequences for teachers. Joe Milwell, who came late to teaching with a good deal of industrial experience, explains teachers' individualism this way:

Teachers generally don't ever act as a group unless the Minister [pressures them], and they suddenly coalesce and act as a group. And the minute the pressure's off, then they fragment again. This is the nature of teaching, whether it's in a staff meeting or whether it's as a complete profession. This is the nature of the beast. *Are you suggesting that a teacher is in a sense an isolate?* Yes. Because he's professionally bound up in what he's doing in his classroom. This would be different in an open space school. But in a 24×24 type of environment like we've got here, yes. That teacher couldn't care less what's happening next to him, unless it's upsetting his class. So becomes an individualist.

There are other sources of the streak of individualism in teachers' ideology; but there is still a lot of force in what he says. The classroom separates teachers from each other in the ordinary course of their work.

As Joe remarks, the classroom is not the only setting for

teaching. A few new high schools, and quite a lot of new primary schools, are built on 'open space' principles. In older schools too there are other spaces. Andy Gallea, the one teacher we met who does no talk-and-chalk at all, has no blackboard because he is a physical education teacher and does all his teaching in the school gym, on the oval, in the nets, on the netball court. He has a rather different relationship with the kids, much more relaxed and equal, than his colleagues in main-stream academic subjects, and criticises them for not being 'prepared to listen to the kids'. Some of this is due to an except-ionally relaxed personal style (feet-on-the-chair and lairy T-shirts), but some is also due in a quite simple way to the different setting of his work. It does not lead him to romanticise the kids ('bloody kids are liars, towards teachers... It really shits me') but it does give him a different angle of view.

Teachers of academic subjects also interact with kids outside the classroom, in the contexts of clubs, sporting events, excur-sions and so on. Not all of this is sweetness and light. Phyllis Howell, the deputy quoted at the start of this section, tells against herself the story of the Great Geography Excursion Disaster a few years back. It had been poorly organised by some-one outside the school who did not understand kids' needs. The accompanying teachers were 'too polite', and under the tight rein the girls went berserk: some shop-lifted, some sniffed glue or took pills. By the last morning of the trip,

> ... all we need is someone to have a fit. Knock on the door.
> 'Miss, Frieda is having a fit'.

On other occasions, however, it can be a revelation. The teachers at Rockwell High organise end-of-year camps, and Arlette Anderson, a domestic science teacher who by no means takes a starry-eyed view of her charges, went away with a group who were about to leave school from Year 10. 'And they were not the same girls.' The ones she had expected to rely on faded into the background; and the girls were organised and pulled into line by 'this real tarty-looking piece' who had never seemed a leader in the classroom. Arlette tells of another camp which included one of two girls who had been her 'arch-enemies' all year, constantly hassling her. In the camp, she found this girl entirely different, happy, able to confide, 'like I was her mother all week'. Back at school after the Christmas break, Arlette expected a new leaf—and it was absolute hell for a year. Then, with the next Christmas approaching, the arch-enemy remembered the next camp, and suddenly became an angel again.

The constraints on their work teachers most often refer to are class sizes and school timetables. Class size both directly defines the teacher's task in whole-class teaching, and limits the teacher's ability to pursue alternatives such as one-to-one work on learning problems. Faye Taylor, a sharply observant maths teacher in one of the working-class schools, notes sadly of a pupil who was not doing 'steady work' in her classes (he was in fact resisting schooling generally at the time):

> I haven't done a very good job on Michael. But you must remember that I had quite a few others leaping around at the same time.

Thus class size has an impact on teachers' stress levels and job satisfaction. The collective memory of our interviewees includes the boom days of the late 1950s, when Ralph Duffy first came to Greenway High to teach science. He expected classes to be smaller than the 55-in-a-room at the primary school where he had been teaching before. They were not.

> I took them into the lab: they were perched around on the window sills, you know, they couldn't all sit down.

Things are better now; but they are not equal. Smaller class sizes, and hence easier teaching, is a common reason given by teachers in the elite private schools for preferring to be there rather than in the state system.

The other great engine of constraint is the device that distributes people into those classrooms, the school timetable. In the typical secondary school, classes are organised in about 40-minute 'periods'; at the end of each period, teachers and taught move on to another encounter. There are various modifications to this, but for the most part the classrooms and time-slots form a mighty grid through which both the school's teaching staff and their clients circulate during the week, in opposite directions.

The constraints that govern the construction of the timetable are formidable. Perhaps 800 kids and 70 teachers have to be fitted in (more in many schools), allowing for the subject specialisations of each of the teachers; the agreed curriculum for the kids; the allowed teacher:pupil ratios in different grades and

different subjects; the use of specialised space or equipment in
practical subjects, sciences, language labs, and physical education; the industrial agreements that lay down the number of
'free' periods in which a teacher is supposed to do marking,
preparation, and individual consultation; choice of options by
the kids; streaming, setting, or other ways the school sorts a
cohort into classes; differential loads for heads of departments
and teachers given special responsibilities outside the classroom;
and so on. Making the timetable is traditionally the job of the
deputy principal, and takes weeks of work at the beginning of
each year. Often the mathematics staff are called in to help; and
some schools have been trying, with varying success, to get the
job onto computers. It is hardly surprising that once a year's
timetable has gelled, no school looks kindly on any proposal to
change it.

Teachers certainly experience it as an absolute constraint on
their work. When the bell goes the kids go, no matter what is
happening, educationally, at the time. The whole school would
seize up otherwise. The 40-minute period becomes a frame
governing all technique. Sheila Goffman (chapter 1) remarks that
by the time you get all the desks shifted around and the kids
settled for a group discussion, half the period has gone. Arlette
Anderson has her version of the same problem:

> The biggest problem here is just keeping the kids quiet for five
> minutes so you can actually tell them what you're going to do that
> lesson. By the time you've done that, 25 minutes of the lesson's
> gone.

Doris Willoughby, a skilful and experienced teacher, is having
trouble getting to know the kids in her 'home class' this year.
There are 37 of them, and the timetable allocates her just five
periods a week with them. Ralph Duffy is supposed to administer 'pastoral care' to a classroom full of teenagers; the timetable gives him ten minutes with them every morning, so he
reads out notices. Doris Willoughby also notes more subtle
effects of the timetable. It makes it difficult for any one teacher
to teach a subject right through the school, from Year 7 to Year
12, which is important if you are to understand the way it is
learnt. And it makes it extremely difficult to follow kids up
systematically, as they are re-sorted and assigned to different
teachers in subsequent years.

It is no wonder that the timetable confronts working teachers like a mountain, massive and immovable. And in one sense it is. But in another sense it is quite a particular solution to the problem of organising the working lives of so many teachers and so many kids. The solution that is more or less standard in Australian secondary schools is dominant for quite specific reasons, including a particular set of divisions among teachers, a particular relation between universities and the curriculum in secondary schools, a particular conception of the process of learning, a particular pattern of control in the education system and of industrial politics on the part of teacher unions. Other patterns are conceivable, and are from time to time tried out: Middleton's *Marking Time* is an important example. Yet no-one who has once been ruled by a high school timetable, either as a teacher or as pupil, will imagine it being revolutionised with lightning speed.

The craft of teaching

Given their situations, how do secondary teachers actually do the job? Many of their practices are versions of a method well adapted to the classroom situation, based on the idea of collective instruction. Here is a brief account of it from a private school history teacher, Julius Abernethy:

> We've just sort of gone through McIntosh, the textbook. We just get them to read round the class and various things. And then I might just elaborate on it; and they'll discuss it if they want to.

Most of the essentials are here. The content to be learnt is decided in advance of the lesson, by the teacher; in this case, on the authority of the textbook. All the kids in the room are expected to learn the same material at the same time; there is to be only one focus of attention in the room, and the teacher may criticise any pupil whose attention wanders. The material is expounded by the teacher—in Julius' classroom in two steps, directed reading followed by his own commentary—and then worked over by the kids. The distinctly subordinate place of the kids' initiative is clearly indicated by Julius' phrasing, 'they'll discuss it if they want to'.

Learning how to do this is acquiring the basic skill in high school teaching as it is presently constituted. A teacher who can do this can at least survive in almost all situations the school throws up.

It sounds easy; in fact it is not. It usually takes at least a year of full–time practice, on top of a year or more of teacher training and some years' advanced study of the subject being taught, before a teacher is any good at it. This is a major reason for the trauma of the First Year Out. Margaret Blackall's eloquent description of adjustment after that experience (p. 16) shows her settling into the standard classroom technique, which requires a certain social distance between teacher and taught, a controlled rapport ('friendly but firm'), a good deal of prior organisation, and—as Margaret honestly remarks—a touch of professional insensitivity.

Some beginners never do get on top of this method, and they are likely to leave teaching quickly, or be pushed into one of the more marginal specialisations around the school. Those who do, learn also to adapt it to the needs of particular subjects and particular classes. Joe Guaraldi, a biology teacher at Greenway High, lays more stress on the pupil-activity end of it, and is supported by the pattern of teaching in his department:

> I try to avoid situations where I'm in front of the class talking for 30 minutes and write up on the blackboard, and the kids are writing notes for 30 minutes. I try to avoid that—not always successfully. I prefer things where the kids are doing something that they would enjoy doing, and that they can see some value in doing, and they can do in their own pace much more.
> *So how do you organise that?*
> Well, all unit biology works in a group structure. Biology is the only subject that they do that in. So there's much more things in biology where the kids can talk amongst themselves and discuss questions. There are options in biology where the kids pick their options and do it for three or four weeks. There's set work in the option, but they get to pick which option they want.

The 'set work' still provides the framework, clearly enough. Jeremy Hansen, an experienced science teacher at St Paul's College, a private school for boys, lays the emphasis more heavily on this:

> We believe learning's hard work, and there's nothing else to do but try and make it as enjoyable as you can but at the same time point out to the boys that there's only one way to learn that topic my friend, and that's to sit down and learn it, there's no other way.

Teachers acquiring this technique learn various tricks of the trade to make the work more manageable. One trick is to teach from the back of the room, because you can see better from there who is wasting time and who is working. Jeremy Hansen arranges the seating in his classes so that all his 'problem children' are at the front and under his eye; though he notes ruefully that there is still 'friction' at the back of the room.

As time goes on, more complex and subtle aspects of the technique are learnt. Pacing, for instance. Myra Elsborough, a science teacher at Auburn College, a school making a big push in the science-maths area, concentrates on Year 11 and 12 teaching and preparation for the highly competitive Matriculation exams. However she does enough teaching in Year 10 to get to know the girls who will come on to her. She has developed ways of getting them used to 'the very big jump in standards' from Year 10 to Year 11; and has a well–worked–out plan for following up this jump with a gradually increasing pace, and teaching them how to handle it.

It is already clear that there is a range of variation within this classroom technique. At one end of the spectrum, 'teacher talk' is what teaching is really about; Julius Abernethy remarks of discussion among his pupils, 'it's not regular teaching'. Push this rather further, and you come to the teaching technique expounded by Angus Barr in chapter 3, 'drill'. Collective recitation, repetition, rote learning, and doing things exactly by rule, still happen in the schools, especially the more conservative private schools. John Welton, a teacher at one such, cheerfully describes how one of the boys in our sample had to adjust:

> He began here with very little idea of presentation of work, and
> with the institution of things like red lines for margins, and
> red–line headings. He's got books now much better than they
> would have been.

But the climate of professional opinion has changed. Few teachers now would make an issues of red lines for margins, and anyone who did would be regarded in most schools as a bit eccentric. The image of professional good practice nowadays is more of someone like Rosa Marshall (chapter 4), Myra Elsborough, or, at a less sophisticated level, Joe Guaraldi.

At the other end of the spectrum Joe's interest in 'group work' and kids going at 'their own pace' turns into the teaching techniques used by Sheila Goffman (chapter 1) and Jack Ryan (chapter 5). Sheila's practice constantly runs up against, and threatens to overflow, the framework of the school timetable. She is, in consequence, criticised by teachers in other departments for having kids out of the classroom too much, though she defends this on the grounds that it is for activities that will 'develop' them. This is a significant example of the way grass-roots practice generates larger conflict, a theme taken up again in chapter 10.

Broadly speaking, this is the range of methods for teaching mainstream academic subjects that we encountered. In non-academic subjects like art, music, crafts, physical education, 'personal development' (sex education, social education), part of the teaching follows the classroom model. This is the more so as these subjects get assimilated into the framework of testing for academic certification. Angela Ruskin, art teacher at St Helen's College, notes that there is a 'perennial problem' of the girls seeing art as a 'soft option'. But this is changing now it is a Matriculation subject. It is gaining more prestige, and most of the assessment at higher levels is by written tests on the model of the established academic subjects.

Still, art is far from being completely assimilated, and Angela spends most of her time in a workshop situation. Like Terry Petersen (chapter 2) she works alongside her students rather than in front of them, physically showing how to do this or that part of the project each has undertaken. She contrasts the effects of this with the usual classroom interactions. The atmosphere is 'more relaxed', the girls speak their minds more, and they talk more freely about their own interests and concerns. It is not only the girls who get satisfaction here. Angela herself had wanted to be a full-time artist before she became a teacher, and would still like to be. The workshop situation allows her to practice her trade, as (to a lesser extent) it does the qualified carpenter Terry Petersen, and (perhaps to a greater one) the athletic Andy Gallea, physical education teacher and all-round sportsman.

A teacher who survives the baptism of fire, picks up a basic technique, and settles down to a career in the schools, may stick at that first phase of learning and stay with tried and true devices for the rest of a working life. But for more reflective teachers the craft can be continually developed and refined. Alison Chant, a mathematics specialist, is a good example of a teacher who is continually reflecting on her methods and their presuppositions.

Perhaps it takes longer to read, understand, and remember than teachers expect. Kids will do it, but they need *time*. If you really want to know something, teach it; it's over-learned. Teachers forget that.

She notes the emotional problems of girls learning maths, and she notes the emotional problems of the maths teacher too:

You have to face it: teaching anything complicated is an unpleasant experience. Things have to be broken up, and that is unpleasant. It is only when it gets back together that it becomes pleasurable—the things academics just love.

This is refining an existing skill to a very high level. Other teachers acquire new specialisations. Glenn Moncrieff, starting out as a history teacher, became more and more interested in the problems of teaching low-stream kids. He became his school's expert on the question, has put himself through a diploma course and a master's degree in 'mental retardation', and is even contemplating going overseas to take a doctorate in special education. Len Johnson is doing the same kind of thing but without benefit of university. Starting out as an English teacher (p. 70), he became the school's unofficial official photographer, runs the camera club, and is re-training himself as a photography teacher.

In such ways individual teachers develop their craft. The changes cumulate, and the craft itself changes. One example has already been mentioned, the decline of drill and the rising emphasis on the pupil's activity in the process of learning. One aspect of the change, a fashion for 'activity teaching', has not always had happy results. Glenn Moncrieff, when teaching Australian history, decided to have his class re-enact in the school grounds the 1854 defence and capture of the Eureka Stockade on the Victorian goldfields. Main result: one kid with injured leg. Other innovations in method are easier on the nerves. One of the most important in recent years has been the development of audio-visual aids for teaching: records, photographic slides, magnetic tapes, film, and more recently TV, video and stereo recording.

Conscious innovation in method is thus an important fact about the craft of teaching. It can also change in less conscious ways, as a result of wider social changes. Len Johnson, looking back on his fifteen years as a teacher, observes

> Where previously the kids used to just shut up, copy it down and
> regurgitate it, that's gone. If they don't understand it, or it doesn't
> interest them, they'll tell you, now. It suits me better in every way.

Not all teachers like it, but they all have to cope with it. Len's
observation is one example of a very widespread sense, among
the teachers we interviewed, that the conditions in which their
craft was exercised had changed, and that the presuppositions of
older techniques and traditional attitudes no longer held.

The division of labour

Different people do different work; that is a basic fact of industrial organisation, and the education industry is no exception.
The work of the teachers we studied was divided in quite complex ways, governed by several principles that are not always
consistent with each other.

The first pattern is the division of labour crystallised in the
school timetable. The collective teaching obligations of the
school are divided according to the different contents of learning
('subjects'), the age of the student and difficulty of the content
('grades'), the presumed ability of the students, either generally
or in a particular subject ('streams', 'sets'), and a complex set of
rules about how much time, and what blocks of time, particular
subject/grade/set combinations can claim of the pupil's working
week.

This carving-up of the total teaching effort of the school's
staff already embodies some important educational decisions
about what is learnt and under what circumstances. There is an
equally complex set of rules, understandings and agreements
about which teachers will do what bits of the total. Teachers are
very conscious of who does the dishing-out, who has influence
on it, what principles govern it, and are often far from pleased
by the result.

Rosa Marshall (chapter 4) noted how as a new member of
staff she got 'all bottom classes'. This is extremely common, and
not only in state schools. Alan Watson teaches the Year 12 lower
stream in his boys' private school, because the upper stream is
monopolised by a teacher who has been there since 1944, and is
an expert on exam techniques. This pattern is another of the
reasons for the trauma of the first years of teaching. You get the
most difficult classes while you are least experienced.

Rosa Marshall noted another important pattern: in the state school she mentioned, all the subject heads, and the principal, were men. Even at St Margaret's College, a school for girls only, the mathematics teachers were all men. That has now changed, though the head of the science department is still a man, and there are no men at all in the English and social science departments. While the school's policy is officially counter-sexist, and

> the students are encouraged to, sort of, not think in terms of sex roles in choosing their subjects, they still see it operating.

Indeed they do. The sexual division of labour is one of the most conspicuous facts about the teaching workforce, operating between sectors of education as well as within schools. Beyond subject specialisation, general assumptions about masculine and feminine character and capacities also come into play. As Len Johnson notes, with a touch of bitterness, he gets the tougher Year 8-10 classes

> because I'm male, and I'm big, and they dish out to the women— well, better classes. I don't get on too well with the subject master.

Beyond the division of labour in teaching, there is a further division of labour among teachers because of non-teaching work, mainly a division between those who do supervisory work and those who do not. Supervisory work is broadly divided between that related to particular subjects and the departments that teach them—which is allocated to department heads (seniors, subject masters, etc)—and the administration of the school as a whole. These tasks are commonly separated in a quite material way by the architecture of the school. The former is based in departmental staff-rooms scattered around the buildings; the latter in 'the school office' or 'the administration' (there are also ruder terms) where principal, deputies, clerks and typists cluster together around the files and the photocopier, and the school nurse, psychologist and careers adviser may also have rooms.

Subtle and sometimes idiosyncratic patterns further subdivide the supervisory and administrative work of the senior teachers. Jeremy Hansen, though not a department head, has been given a subject master's teaching load in the timetable so he can be his school's Director of Extracurricular Activities. As he puts it, if 'it's not sport and it's not academic, it's mine'. He does anything from setting up a work experience programme to organising flying lessons for senior boys. Margaret Atwill, the only woman among the senior staff of Greenway High, has inform- ally but effectively been landed with the 'problems that involve girls'. She has become the administration's trouble shooter for issues about the emotional and sexual lives of the girls at the school, which are routinely passed over to her—one can almost hear the sighs of relief—by the men: truancies, family dramas, pregnancies, uncontrolled aggression, conflicts with male teachers, and so on and on.

Having got all this nicely laid out, it is now time to take some of it back. The division of labour among teachers is limited in various ways. The distinction between those who do adminis- tration and those who do classroom work is far from absolute. Margaret Atwill, even with that management workload, commonly does ten periods' teaching a week; Terry Petersen (chapter 2) does 24. The distinction may be consciously minimised. Phyllis Howell notes the importance of classroom contact hours for her care–and–maintenance work as deputy, in relation to the other staff as well as the students:

> Some schools I think the administration sort of go beyond it. But I
> think it's important to get the contact, as far as understanding
> what other staff want. I mean, it's that daily contact. You get to
> know one bunch of kids quite well; and you can sense the mood
> of the school in the children you see every day.

The division of labour between departments may also be blurred, not always intentionally. The making of the timetable itself is a force breaking down the division of labour, since the filling up of the slots—especially for the newer teachers who are last in the queue—obliges some people to take classes in subjects outside their own specialty. Roy Clive, in a boys' private school, com- plains that the only gets half his classes in his own subject, and usually with juniors:

> I'd like to spend more time teaching seniors, but I suppose being
> only a junior member of staff I can't really pick and choose. In
> fact even the senior people can't really pick and choose that much.
> Just timetabled.

Doris Willoughby, trained as an english/history teacher, found herself teaching maths and physical education. Lots of teachers had similar stories.

The other important qualification is that the division of labour changes historically. Teachers are the most numerous, but are far from being the only group of workers in schools. As O'Donnell points out in *The Basis of the Bargain*, a good deal of the clerical work once done by teachers has been hived off and assigned to clerks and secretaries, who are now present in schools in considerable numbers. Cleaners, maintenance workers, caretakers, teaching aides, kitchen workers, psychologists, nurses, and others are there too. As with clerical staff, the division of labour between these workers and teachers is not historically fixed.

Nor is the division of labour within teaching, even the 'subject' divisions that seem so firmly institutionalised, quite fixed. At a couple of points in the research we came upon new subject specialisations being constructed. This can be seen most clearly in the story of Andrew Sutting, a maths teacher at Greenway High. He started out teaching maths to lower forms, and science too; gradually he has contracted his teaching to senior maths, where computing is part of the curriculum. He is the school's computer buff. He persuaded the administration to outlay $2000 on a school computer (a small one, but that was quite a chunk of a high school budget at the time); and his declared aim is to get computing, as a basic skill, on the timetable for all students.

In doing this he is not just constructing a personal niche in a particular school. He and teachers like him in other schools are engaged in redefining the division of labour by producing a new school subject. Given that there are already computing departments in the universities which can give it academic respectability, and there is a labour market demand and new technology to give it economic credibility, there is every prospect that they will succeed. And there is every indication, too, that it will be a strongly masculinised subject—given its growth out of mathematics teaching, its association with sophisticated machinery, and its inevitable association with power. As with the impact of computing in industry, discussed by Game and Pringle in *Gender At Work*, the sexual division of labour is recreated as the labour process is transformed.

Summary, chapter 6

Teachers' work can be understood as a particular *labour process* and as governed by a particular *division of labour*. In comparison with other workers, the object of teachers' labour is difficult to specify, so the definition of their task can expand almost without limit, and the work could be intensified indefinitely. But it is governed by strong constraints—such as the nature of the classroom and other settings, class sizes, the timetable—which embody particular social relations and policies. The work of secondary teaching is most often performed by a technique of collective instruction on predetermined content. There are a good many refinements and variations of this technique. Alternatives are most often found in 'practical' subjects, though mainstream technique also changes historically. The timetable embodies a division of labour based on one set of principles, *viz* content, difficulty and pupil age. Teachers' work is also divided in ways reflecting experience, sex, administrative involvement, and the histories of particular schools. All these divisions get blurred in practice, though together they strongly influence the work of any given teacher. The division of labour also changes historically, as in the emergence of new special-isations like computing.

7

The curriculum

As well as being a definition of the pupils' learning, 'the curriculum' is also a definition of the teachers' work. The way it is organised, and the social practices that surround it, have profound consequences for teachers.

The competitive academic curriculum

In all the schools we studied a particular way of organising knowledge and learning was hegemonic. I will call this the 'competitive academic curriculum'. To say it is hegemonic is not to say it is the only curriculum in those schools. It is to say that this pattern has pride of place in the schools, it dominates most people's ideas of what real learning is about; its logic has the most powerful influence on the organisation of the school, and of the education system generally; and it is able to marginalise or subordinate the other curricula that are present.

The competitive academic curriculum has the following main features. First, the knowledge that is to be taught is derived mainly from university-based disciplines like history, mathematics, geography, German, biology. This connection guarantees both its reliability or truth, and its status as significant knowledge, worthy to be taught and learnt. The connection is made concrete in teaching materials, especially textbooks, and in the lives of teachers through their tertiary training. School knowledge retains the academic form of a self-referring, abstract body of knowledge. This strongly separates what is learned from the personal and social experiences of the learner.

Second, this knowledge is organised hierarchically, from less difficult to more difficult, from basic principles to later elaborations and refinements, from introductory approximations to later precisions, from more concrete to more abstract. Broadly speaking there is one, and only one, path through the material, which all pupils should follow.

Third, the teaching is basically transfer teaching. Something that the teacher already knows is to be transferred to the mind of the pupil, who does not yet know it. In principle the whole course of learning can be laid down in advance; with, in practice, variations to accord with the aptitudes and enthusiasm of the pupil.

Fourth, the pupil's learning is organised as the individual appropriation of bits of this knowledge. The fact that a whole class is usually taught as a unit does not affect this in the least, as the pupils are learning in parallel, not in a joint way. Indeed they are learning in competition with each other. When the learning is being assessed, it is how much each of them can reproduce as an individual, not what they can do with it together, that is measured.

Fifth, the knowledge acquired is regularly tested through competitive examination, to determine who of a cohort of students has acquired most and who least. At certain points the results of this testing are publicly certified. The testing strongly influences who is allowed into further formal education, and the certification influences the pupil's position on entry to the labour market. School teachers are recruited mainly from those who have done well in this testing; though pupils who have done extremely well are usually able to go into better-paying professions.

Historically, this pattern was constructed by the meeting of the academic traditions of the pre-war 'grammar school' or selective high school, with the mass clientele created by the postwar expansion of secondary schooling and the growth of credentialism in the labour market. There have been some shifts of emphasis within it. The teaching of Latin and Greek, once dominant, has declined almost to nothing; the classics' place in the sun has been taken by mathematics and the 'hard' sciences, physics and chemistry. Debate continues as to how pure, or how applied, their teaching ought to be. New fields bid for inclusion; I have already mentioned computing as a likely successful challenger. But the broad outlines laid down in the 1940s and 1950s remain, a generation later.

Many teachers are strongly attached to this curriculum. A key reason is their attachment to the knowledge it embodies. Margaret Blackall (chapter 1) remarked 'I'm here mostly because I love my subject so much.' Lorraine Smart, at the same school:

> I'm an academically inclined person myself. I really enjoy the study of literature and poetry, things like this.

Faye Taylor, a maths teacher at the same school, pushes it even further. Her great love is history, and she tried teaching it but shifted to maths because she couldn't bear the way the kids butchered her favourite subject. It is notable that these three teachers come from an ordinary working-class comprehensive high school, not a selective elite school. The attachment to knowledge they express is both real and widespread.

At the same time, many teachers are sharply aware of its cost and disadvantages. Here is Joe Guaraldi, who himself teaches an academic subject:

> *What's the main mode of teaching here?*
> Well, the main mode of teaching here is sort of chalk-and-talk.
> *Yet it obviously produces results?*
> Academic results, yes. Yes, I guess it does. It also produces some attitudes with kids that I don't like to see. The only aim of being at school is to get your pass and get out... The school likes to say that it's got a function of inculcating social values in kids. But in practice, I think, that's all completely subdued to the academic aims of the school. And this school is completely academic, has very little obvious sort of social values that it deliberately tries to impart. Except as gets imparted accidentally through the way it works; kids pick up values simply from what goes on. Things like: to get away with what you can is the main thing to do; and get out and get a job is the most important thing; and get an A grade because it will help you get a job. That's the sort of things that they learn, the social values that they learn, in a school like this. I don't really like a school like this.

The competitiveness and selfishness encouraged by this way of doing things is both clear and offensive to Joe.

The other major criticism repeatedly made by teachers is that the competitive academic curriculum suits some kids, but alienates others—perhaps most. They are right.

Rosa Marshall's account of her difficulties teaching in a state school (chapter 4) showed the curriculum as a *barrier* between the teacher and the class, preventing her from constructing the kind of relationship with the kids in which effective teaching could occur. She made a practical critique of the curriculum: she resigned. Len Johnson is another making a practical critique, re–training himself as a photography teacher—because the kids like it, and that is 'a crucial difference'. He numbers himself among the 'fair proportion' of teachers at his school who think that

> kids need to be treated as kids rather than as receptacles for
> knowledge.

The ways an academically organised curriculum alienates and eventually excludes the majority of kids have been traced out in *Making the Difference*, and need not be laboured here. What still need to be stressed are the consequences for teachers.

Sorting people

One of the most important effects is the pressure it sets up to test, grade, and stream the kids. Not that this is entirely a new idea. Plato's Republic was to be ruled by a somewhat humourless bunch of psychometricians:

> Therefore the first and most important of God's commandments to
> the Rulers is that they must exercise their function as Guardians
> with particular care in watching the mixture of metals in the
> characters of the children. If one of their own children has bronze
> or iron in its make-up, they must harden their hearts, and degrade
> it to the ranks of the industrial and agricultural class where it
> properly belongs. Similarly, if a child of this class is born with
> gold or silver in its nature, they will promote it appropriately to be
> a Guardian or an Auxiliary. For they know that there is a
> prophecy that the State will be ruined when it has Guardians of
> silver or bronze.[2]

The competitive academic curriculum makes the sorting, and the hardening of hearts, a central reality of contemporary school life.

In doing that, it creates a massive dilemma for teachers. Most of them do not need researchers to tell them that the testing and streaming system has ill-effects on school life. I have quoted Joe Guaraldi's criticism of the way the kids come to believe that the aim of learning is to 'get an A grade'; and (in chapter 1) Margaret Blackall's heartbreaking recollection of her first two

days at Greenway High watching the kids getting tested and
sorted into 'the dummy class'. Clive Brimcombe, a private
school teacher, tells of the introduction of a system of reporting
which sharpened up the competitiveness of the system, comparing each child's percentage mark with the average mark for
the whole year, and of its degrading and destructive impact on
some of the kids. He left that school. These stories could be
multiplied.

A streaming system also has an impact on the teachers. Mary
Coleman, who supports the policy of streaming, still notes:

> The thing of course that's wrong with that, is that someone's got
> to get the bottom stream!

which means 'a vast amount of discipline problems'. Teaching
the lower classes in a streamed school is a stressful and often
extremely unrewarding business. At its worst, it involves confrontation and physical violence—the cane on one side, occasional physical assaults on teachers on the other. At its best,
most teachers regard it as a kind of purgatory and try to avoid it
if possible. Since they are more able to do this as they advance
in their career, the tendency is for the older, more experienced,
and more influential staff to get the more agreeable teaching.
The negative effects of the streaming system are thus to some
extent screened out at the decision-making levels of the school
hierarchy.

Though that is one reason the streaming system survives, there
is a more important one. The alternative is unstreamed classes:
and they have problems too. Phyllis Howell, the deputy who
insists that 'you have to like kids', was formerly a strong critic
of streaming, and still is against 'the streaming mentality' which
ensures failure and puts people into categories. She managed to
persuade her school, which was introducing a new social science
curriculum, to introduce unstreamed classes. But too many
problems were caused. 'Behaviour problems' arose because of
the frustration of mixed abilities being taught together. The top
ability kids needed 'more reward'. The school, and Phyllis,
abandoned the experiment; subjects are now individually
streamed ('setting'). Mary Coleman, despite the reservation just
quoted, agrees. Kids are not 'equal', and you cannot teach them
as if they were.

For many teachers, especially in the private schools, this view

is so much a matter of common sense that it virtually goes without saying. The difference in abilities is a fact of life. If you
have a mixed-ability class and teach at the pace of the slowest,
the most able kids get frustrated and bored. This is unfair to the
talented. If you teach at the pace of the fastest, the less able kids
get left behind. For both, the solution is to divide the group.
And within limits, streaming works. It does allow faster-paced,
more stimulating teaching with the academic stars. And if it
concentrates the dumber kids in classes that are bound to be
difficult, at least it makes possible a modified version of the
curriculum more adapted to their slower pace or limited
intellectual abilities.

So runs the argument. It misses two vital things. One is the
politics of the situations where unstreamed classes have been
tried, as in Phyllis Howell's experiment: generally, introduced in
the face of scepticism and resistance, lacking support staff and
relevant training, short on appropriate and varied materials. The
other, more subtle but perhaps more basic, is the question of
where these conceptual categories of ability and pace, this unit of
teaching, and this conception of learning, actually come from.
They do not fall from the sky. To anticipate the more systematic discussion of teachers' knowledge in chapter 11, I would
argue that they arise from particular educational practices;
specifically that they are generated by, or at least strongly shaped
by, the competitive academic curriculum. It is the kids' ease and
skill with this particular organisation of learning that is constantly at issue in the 'streaming' debates. To the extent that the
school defines its offer of teaching in terms of this curriculum,
'mixed ability' becomes a problem and streaming a resolution of
it. The connections are so close that streaming can virtually be
regarded as the institutionalised form of the competitive
academic curriculum. It is very difficult to run that sort of
curriculum without a streamed school.

Subordinated curricula

In the timetable are fragments of curricula organised in other
ways. Their main home is in the 'subjects' which do much of
their teaching outside conventional classrooms, such as physical
education, manual arts (craft, technics, technical studies) art
and music.

The most obvious difference from the competitive academic

curriculum is that in all these cases a main aim of teaching is a particular bodily skill or set of skills. Andy Gallea describes his physical education teaching in these terms:

What do you do with them?
Oh, it varies, you know. Well, 10th year is a sort of—how we base our sporting or PE year, what we try to do is, First and Second Form is based entirely on skills. Third Form is a sort of transition period, where you're starting to go from school work into recreation work, and just giving them an idea of what sports are available; playing sports, teaching them the skills of the sport, and just letting them know that there are these sports available around, this sort of stuff.

As with the workshop learning in manual arts, the central process of learning is by the direct exercise of the skill involved; and the main aim is the development of a *common competence*, rather than competitively ranked performances. (Which is not to deny that there is a competitive element in much school sport. There is, but it does not provide the underlying rationale for PE teaching.) Andy's comments also point to another difference, this time in the intellectual content of his subject. The point of the information transfer he describes in Third Form is not to start the students on the elementary steps of a hierarchically organised body of knowledge, but to give all of them the *information necessary for practice*; in this case, acquainting them with 'what sports are available'.

A third point of difference is that these subjects build much more directly on *student interest* than academic subjects do. In craft and art teaching this means producing pieces of work which have an intrinsic value for the student. Most of the time this is seen by the teachers as one of the great advantages of their subjects, a guarantee of student involvement; though it can also be felt as a constraint by teachers whose own enthusiasms do not coincide with their students'. Angela Ruskin, now at a private school, at one stage was teaching art in a state school with a working-class clientele. 'You have to be much more matter-of-fact' with those kids, she remarks; and to illustrate, explains that her main success with them was when she taught them how to print T-shirts emblazoned with their favourite pop groups, the Eagles and the Bay City Rollers. Angela is much more interested in the fine arts than in what she calls 'fabric crafts', and is much better suited by the genteel atmosphere and 'civilised' clientele of St Helen's College for Girls.

The subordination of these curricula is manifest in their generally low prestige among teachers. Theo Georges, a young manual arts teacher, comments on the discrepancy between the way the kids react to it and the way the teachers do:

What sort of regard does Manual Arts have as a faculty in the school?
Well, amongst the children, very highly.
Why's that?
I don't know. Maybe they achieve more there, through our means and methods. The children, fairly high. Amongst the staff, it's one of these, you know, 'If you've got brains then you can't do manual arts', and vice versa.
Is that true?
I don't think it is. I mean [pointing to a piece of carpentry] we had a student that made a desk like this last year. Instead of making the rail parallel he had it going down on an incline. Now that takes brains to work that out, that thing's got to go level, and work out exactly what it's got to fit into. And the thing doesn't come just like that because you've practiced it for so many years.
That means manual arts can be a field in which people can be intelligent and creative—but is it?
Oh yes. Well, is it? See we're fairly limited in what we can do because of the time. People think, 'Oh, bloody hand skills and all this sort of rubbish doesn't cultivate the mind'.
Who?
Well, I imagine art people—the English people—and the head himself.

What Theo is saying, put more formally, is that manual arts does not lack an intellectual content but organises it in a different way. Where the academic curriculum strongly separates mental from manual labour, the learning of principles from the application of skills, this kind of curriculum unifies them. That is a major reason for its popularity with the kids, a popularity that extends to kids in general, not just the 'less able'. But, as Theo also stresses, there can be no doubt about its place on the school's totem pole. And it is notable that the put-down Theo suffers is couched in the characteristic language of the competitive academic curriculum, the little ideology of 'brains'.

It is also interesting that Theo notes art teachers among those who look down on manual arts. There is a significant difference here among non–academic subjects. Some have their own claims to cultural prestige, their own strings leading to the great world.

Art is one; music is another. In both cases there are down-market versions—rock music, Bay City Rollers T-shirts—and fine arts versions. Teachers have to strike their own balance between mass appeal and cultural prestige.

New curricula

Just as innovation in technique is part of the picture of teaching practice, so it is with curriculum. A number of the teachers we talked to were involved with new curricula currently bidding for a place in the school's programme, though still marginalised by the mainstream academic curriculum.

First are curricula which are bidding for a place *in* the competitive academic framework, though they have not yet won it. Computing is the clearest example we came across in the fieldwork. Some 'new' social sciences, like political science and sociology, are also being levered into senior school timetables as conventional courses with university-knowledge-based syllabuses, formal individual assessment, and so on. The novelty is in the content, not the form or method. Joe Guaraldi makes a pungent comment on this process as it operates in his school:

> The trouble with a lot of courses like that, social education courses, is that they set out to be of benefit to students. But the way they are taught in strict—I don't really know how they should be taught—but I just get the feeling that the way they're taught at the moment the kids don't see the benefit. A lot of those courses are meant to rock them; therefore they don't have the benefit they should have.

The second kind of curriculum is linked to the academic mainstream in a different way. The process of streaming always raises questions about what kind of learning is appropriate for the lower streams. The increased retention rates of the 1970s, combined with massively increased youth unemployment, have forced this issue on the secondary schools. In a number of the schools we studied an anxious debate was under way about whether to introduce alternative curricula for non-academic kids, and if so, what their content and shape should be.

In the working-class schools some of the debate was focussed on early leavers. At Rockwell High, for instance, Sheila Goffman (chapter 1) was one of a group of teachers working out a program for Year 10 kids that would stress 'education for survival': how to cope with unemployment, how to get jobs, how to pool their experience, and so on. Arlette Anderson saw the key problem rather differently:

> The biggest problem we have with the kids here, the ones who are bright, is they get to Year 10 and everyone's sort of leaving, I even see it now with my Year 10s this year, the ones who are staying, all the other ones knock them. 'Oh, how could you stay here for another two years!' They really give them a bad time. And so a lot of them actually leave. And of course the bright ones all get jobs, and don't come back.

In short, the traditional selection process within the school has been disrupted by the recession. How generally this is true is a debatable point; but it is at least clear that working out a non-academic program for Year 11-12, traditionally the exclusive preserve of the competitive academic curriculum, has become a pressing issue.

We were surprised to find that a parallel debate was going on inside some of the private schools too. At St Margaret's College, for instance, the staff is split. In a private school the issue inevitably takes the form of a debate about the school's positioning in the market. Rosa Marshall, as noted in chapter 4, argues for continuing to do what the school does best; others argue that too academic an emphasis narrows the school's potential clientele and weakens its market position. Others again are divided within themselves. Phyllis Howell is one. She knows that non-academic students have ideas, and much to contribute; she regrets the high formal expectations placed on them.

> They're good people and good citizens but they're made to feel inferior. It's a pity more kids don't leave, and find something they can do and fit in with, rather than struggle through to Year 12.

It is a measure of the intransigence of the issue that so energetic and imaginative a teacher as Phyllis Howell is left wishing weakly that the kids would solve the problem for her by going away.

The third kind of curriculum is in some ways the most interesting, because it is developed in conscious opposition to the hegemonic curriculum. For the same reason it lives a fugitive life on the fringes of the official programme, and is often difficult to document and describe.

Mary Coleman studied social science at university, and is convinced of the importance of teaching working-class kids about the real political world. She finds their political ignorance and apathy 'fairly horrifying', and the existing curricula irrelevant. So she is building lots of contemporary-issues material into her history and English lessons, and is currently trying to get her department head to agree to a 'Modern World' (contemporary history) course. Clive Brimcombe has very similar ideas. He taught in a progressive private school, which among other things used to get in speakers from the political parties; Clive himself constructed and taught an 'Australian Studies' course which looked at the social and political issues of the day. But in this case the private-school market mechanism operated against progressive reform: parents withdrew support, the school got 'scared stiff', in Clive's phrase, and rapidly withdrew into formal pedagogy and assessment.

The key point in both Mary's and Clive's thinking is not so much the kids' expressed interests (both have in fact run into serious resistance from the kids they are teaching) as their *need to know*. In this respect the logic is like that already noted in physical education. Competitive assessment is in principle irrelevant; a common competence is the educational goal.

Other teachers have been working up programmes with a much greater stress on the kids' interests and participation. Sheila Goffman's version of English, discussed in chapter 1, is a case in point. Drama workshops, debating, writing projects and encounter-group exercises are mixed in with the more conventional subject-matter, and provide a vehicle for discussing personal interests, family problems, peer-group relationships. The curricular principles here are a bit more difficult to formulate, but two at least seem important. First, the kids' own *experience and relationships* are taken as a major source of curriculum content. In some basic sense, the curriculum is grown organically from the situation, rather than being laid down in advance either by academic authority (as in the mainstream curriculum) or by teachers' judgments of what the kids need to know. Second, the importance of *motivation and interest* in learning is stressed to the point where this becomes a test of the relevance of curriculum content. What the kids are not interested in is not taught.

This can, of course, become a rather flexible criterion. A skilful teacher will find ways of interesting students in a very wide range of material, including a good deal of the classic academic content. Nevertheless this is the point on which a lot of teachers reject Sheila Goffman's pedagogy and that of other 'progressive' colleagues. Margaret Atwill is one who finds such ideas an affront to her dignity as a teacher and to the mission of the school as an agent of enlightenment:

> I don't think that I could be involved with a scheme that was simply entertaining or filling in time of students. I don't know that I see school as a place of hunting around for something that will interest them, and to provide for filling in their time. Now maybe there's a place for this to be done somewhere, but I don't see myself fitting into that pattern. Not as an entertainment to begin with!

Not that Margaret lacks concern with the issues Sheila is dealing with, nor that she opposes having controversial issues discussed in class. But she is acutely concerned that teachers should do so in a balanced and 'tactful' way, and wants to be sure that current-affairs material does not 'break into' the syllabus too much and crowd out the regular content. In short, she wants to keep these alternative curricula firmly marginalised. Since she is twice Sheila's age and a deputy principal, her views carry some weight.

Curriculum dynamics

As Margaret Atwill's remarks imply, the various curricula do not sit side-by-side in the schools. They exist in definite relationships with each other, often involving tension between teachers. These relationships change over time, often as a result of shifts and conflicts among teachers. Several dynamics of curriculum change are apparent in our interviews.

The first is a direct consequence of the hegemony of the competitive academic curriculum. Marginalised curricula can gain space, status and resources in the schools by redefining themselves as part of the hegemonic curriculum. The process is like the 'Sanskritisation' of upwardly mobile castes in India; to register their arrival and claim prestige, they adopt more and more Brahmin social customs and religious observances.

The pressure on a marginalised subject to attempt this can be quite serious. The contempt of academic teachers, registered by Theo Georges for manual arts (p. 94), is not an easy thing to handle; nor is the experience registered by Terry Petersen (p. 31), of repeatedly seeing your best students leave your field because they would lose out academically if they continued with it. So the transformation of woodwork and metalwork into technics, cooking and sewing into domestic science, is not accidental; though neither of these fields has taken the process nearly as far as art (p. 80).

The second is an evolution going on within the hegemonic curriculum itself. In a number of ways the definition of content and method has become less settled. The authority of the centrally-defined official syllabus, once almost absolute, has declined drastically. Individual schools are responsible for more of the content and more of the assessment, even in highly academic subjects. Options within subjects have multiplied. Choice between subjects has also grown, with the decline of across-the-board streaming and its replacement by setting within subjects.

These developments give more responsibility to teachers, and in that respect correspond to the image of increasing profession-alisation. They also create more work, and more emotional pressure on teachers as they are thrown more onto their own resources.

The days when you could teach a new subject at a day's notice by pure craft technique, reading the text and following the syllabus, keeping one chapter ahead of the class until the exams came round, are gone. That system, especially with the external exams, made the kids responsible for the outcome, after the teacher had done a standard job of presenting the standard syllabus. In the new situation it is much less clear what is the teacher's fault and what is not. Teachers are pushed to take more responsibility for the kids' learning, and have more to fear if it goes wrong—in terms of their own self-esteem if nothing else. Teachers, in short, are made more vulnerable. That vulner-ability is a strong motive for many to resist further change in these directions.

Yet these changes have not been incidental, any more than the emergence of the 'new curricula' noted in the last section. Both have been responses to deep-seated problems in the competitive academic curriculum. That curriculum, despite its remarkable success in the last generation, contains at least two important contradictions, which surface as practical dilemmas for the schools.

The first is between the academic content and the competitive organisation of learning and assessment. The hegemonic curri-

culum is tied at one end to the world of academic knowledge, at
the other to the labour market and the production of credentials.
Their demands are often in tension. How broadly to follow an
intellectual argument, how narrowly to prepare for the exams, is
a standard dilemma of teaching. The issue can be posed more
grandly. I have quoted Margaret Blackall's statement that
'schools are to pass on knowledge', and that we shouldn't be
'channelling people into boxes' (p. 17). The interview goes on:

Do you think the school does that at the moment?
It does; but it has got pressure from the outside. It's what parents
always want. Very few parents will talk about how good knowledge
is, or school aims other than finding jobs. Parents will say, 'look,
you make him do well because he's got to get a good job'. Or
'I'm with you too, but you know you've got to make him do well
so he can get a good job'. And I come under heavy fire all the
time because I'm teaching a subject that doesn't have any
utilitarian values. I argue this question of knowledge and it just
goes over their heads.

In Margaret's view, the two sides of the contradiction are
attached to two distinct groups: the teachers talk knowledge and
Aims of Education, the parents talk jobs. Other teachers make
similar comments. As we argued in *Making the Difference*, this
is a misunderstanding of the parents: their concern about jobs is
real, but there is also a real respect for knowledge as such to be
found in working-class communities. Nor are teachers as a group
unconcerned with their pupils' job prospects. Jack Ryan (chapter
5) takes it furthest, but many other teachers appreciate what he
is doing. Yet the conditions of teachers' work, and of parents'
communication with them, make these facts about each group
difficult for the other to see. Thus one consequence of the
hegemonic curriculum is an easily aroused mistrust between the
two groups of adults most concerned with working-class kids'
education.

The other prominent contradiction has to do with the abstractness of academic knowledge. This is the source of some of the
real virtues of the hegemonic curriculum, not least its intellectual
power and capacity for critique. Abstraction allows transcen-
dence of the immediate situation, comparison of the real with
the possible, critical reflection on current practice. The techniques of argument and research acquired in academic subjects
give access to a much wider world of thought and knowledge

than the immediate content studied. These are things that academically oriented teachers value, and rightly so. They are among the things that working-class people sought in the crucial period of the 1940s and 1950s when they demanded wider access to secondary and higher education, and accepted academic definitions of its content.

Yet that abstractness is also experienced by many kids and teachers as a barrier to communication and understanding, and to the intellectual growth it is supposed to encourage. When Angela Ruskin, the art teacher, complained that 'you have to be much more matter-of-fact' with the kids in a working-class school, she was groping for words for this issue. Its class dimension has been a main theme of educational sociology in recent decades.[3] The obvious discomfort of masses of working-class kids with a programme that presents itself to them in conventional academic terms has been a principal motive for the curriculum reform movement of the last fifteen or twenty years.

This movement is, perhaps, the final point to be registered here. The period has seen, as well as increasing stress and doubt about directions, an unprecedented flowering of teachers' creativity and invention. Teachers have gone to work on the curriculum and have produced new content (whole new subject-matters as well as re-organising existing subjects and connecting them to kids' lives), new assessment methods (ranging from simpler ways of recording assessments to non-competitive and goal-based assessment), and new relationships between teachers and the curriculum (from designing small units of work to accepting responsibility for the curriculum's fundamental nature).[4]

This process has constantly run up against the entrenched authority of the competitive academic curriculum. It has so far not produced an alternative which commands wide assent and is a serious challenger for hegemony in the school system; though a good many individual schools have reworked their programmes. Many teachers, in consequence, feel blocked or trapped. This can be taken as one sign of a crisis in the relationship between the schools and a large part of their clientele, which has been precipitated by the collapse of the youth labour market. A crisis is precisely a situation in which there is no easy way out.

The drift of conservative policy in this situation has been towards splitting the curriculum: refurbishing the competitive academic program for some (*inter alia* syphoning more money into private schools and increasing the selectiveness of the public schools), and creating a residual, more or less vocational, curriculum for the rest. That has some attractions for teachers, and some very obvious dangers—not least, a splitting of the teaching profession along the same lines. What reasons teachers might have to support a democratic resolution of the problems will be considered in chapter 12.

Summary, chapter 7

The hegemonic curriculum is based on a hierarchy of academic knowledge and organises the pupil's learning in the form of individual competition. Teachers are attached to academic knowledge for several good reasons, but this curriculum creates serious difficulties in their working lives, especially through its close connection with the practices of certification and streaming. There are also curricula organised in different ways in the more 'practical' subjects with a closer connection between experience, knowledge and practice, though with less prestige in the schools. New curricula bidding for a place in the schools' program include new academic fields, alternative curricula for 'non-academic' students, and political and experiential curricula constructed in opposition to the hegemonic pattern. The relationships between these curricula are constantly under negotiation among teachers. Several dynamics of curriculum change appear: the 'sanskritisation' of marginal fields, decentralisation of control in academic subjects, and the working out of contradictions in the hegemonic curriculum between content and form and about the abstractness of knowledge. A conscious curriculum reform movement is now an important part of educational politics, though its directions remain open.

8

Relationships with kids

Discipline and control

When Arlette Anderson came to Rockwell High, her first post, she went through the classic blooding of a new teacher in a working-class school. Your educational ideals, she recalls, are 'smashed out of you in the first month'. The kids do not want to learn, and the teacher is steadily demoralised: 'You try your hardest to put a stimulating lesson together, and the kids just sit and stare at you'. When they aren't sitting and staring, they are running riot: 'so undisciplined, so noisy, so rude'. Within a day or two, one of the boys had offered her a direct sexual insult: 'Why haven't you got a boyfriend—is there something wrong with you?' Arlette observes she could not have said that to her teachers in a pink fit, and she came from a school that was considered tough.

Arlette is nobody's doormat, and she bounced back, tackling the kids about their sexism, and becoming, in her own words, 'a very autocratic teacher'. She runs her lessons, she remarks wryly, like a sergeant-major: 'The kids almost salute me now.'

She has found she cannot do discussions and debates in this situation. 'I've tried all that'. Even a simple role-playing exercise needed months of preparation.

> You can't really go in for innovative teaching unless the kids are sort of intelligent, they can read and write, they are cooperative—not even so much to you but to one another. [But] they all fight between one another. And you find in the end you just get back to talk-and-chalk and textbook teaching, because you just can't be bothered going through the hassle all the time.

Arlette's story is worth comparing with those of Sheila Goffman, Margaret Blackall, and Rosa Marshall in chapters 1

103

and 4. They point both to the enormous practical importance of 'discipline' for teachers, and to the difficulty of bringing it to focus as a single issue. It has to do with teacher training, with the sexual politics of schools, with teaching method, with teachers' self-esteem, and with the social class relations operating in schooling. It is this complex net of connections that makes 'discipline' issues constantly seem to dissolve into something else, and repeatedly frustrates official inquiries and policy-making bodies that try to deal with them as narrowly-defined issues of rule-breaking and punishment.

There is every reason to think the problematic character of discipline is built into the very structure of mass schooling. Certainly some teachers see it that way. Joe Guaraldi at Greenway High is one. He offers his analysis when talking about kids' resistance to control in school, and though it is not couched in an academic language, it is the more vivid for that:

> Well basically, this is the thing that I've got against this authoritarianism. That teachers are made to feel that—and I guess it's true in a school like this—that if they are not going to be strict with the kids, the kids are going to riot, and go all over them. And so they have to be strict with the kids and sort of authoritarian. And because they are authoritarian, they act—not as a normal adult would act, towards a child that age. And therefore the children don't regard them as a normal adult they would see outside the school grounds.

This is the side of school life that the kids themselves most resent: being shouted at, ordered about, sometimes being hit; being regimented, lined up, marched about; being shut up when they want to talk, made to be active when they want to be still; being subject all the time to arbitrary dealing by the teachers which they often experience as 'unfairness'; being picked on, criticised, sometimes sworn at, and subject to a range of sanctions and punishments at the teacher's will.

Some teachers make a very public point of imposing this regime. Arlette Anderson—'the kids almost salute me now'— does it reluctantly. Alan Watson, a teacher at a private school, does it with a cheerful brutality that suggests no reservations at all:

> My general philosophy is that in First Form you terrify them so much that it takes them six years before they realise that you're at all human.

He compares it happily to the training of puppies—a bit of intimidation is useful—though he tries to mix the fear with a bit of 'friendliness'. Like Alan, a number of other teachers told us how to impose discipline on meeting a new class. The recipe commonly involved coming down hard in the first week; punishing a couple of kids, no matter who, for any offences, no matter how small; and then when they are under control, easing up in the following weeks.

Joe Guaraldi is right; this is not as a normal adult would act. And the result is, exactly as he says, that the kids do not treat the teachers as normal adults. Arlette herself spells out a striking example of the consequences. Because she is a manual-arts teacher she gets to hear more of the kids' discussion of personal relationships than most, and she therefore knows that many of the girls ignore contraception. The school set up special classes about sex and contraception. They don't work. Arlette heard one girl tell her girlfriends that her older sister had told her, 'Don't go on the pill, it screws up your insides and later on you can't have any babies'. The girls, Arlette says, will believe a mother, or a virgin aunt, or a sister. They will not believe the scientific information they are given in the special classes, as she pointed out to the teacher in charge, 'because you are a teacher'. The curriculum breaks down because there is no trust.

But Joe is right only in a limited sense. Teachers act differently from 'normal adults' because normal adults do not have to deal with kids in the circumstances in which teachers work. Without condoning the attitudes or practices of genuinely authoritarian characters, it is important to recognise that the disciplinary responses of teachers in general are intelligible and reasonable responses to situations they have been presented with, over which they have (in the short term) limited control, and in which they often have little room to manoeuvre. Arlette Anderson, I think, is closer to the norm. She is a lively, free-thinking, in some ways radical person, far from being a petty despot. She has learnt to boss the kids about because it is the only way she could survive as a teacher in the circumstances she found herself in.

How are those circumstances shaped, in the working-class secondary school? The first fact is a considerable amount of alienation, passive resistance, and active disruption on the part of the kids, especially those in lower streams, sets, or non-academic 'tracks'. This confronts the individual teacher as a given. Nothing she or he can do will make much difference to it; it is basically a question of how to come to terms with it. The pressures from the kids themselves are contradictory. On the one hand there is a demand to relax controls, be easy-going, give them space, have a joke. Many teachers spoke of this pressure: Len Johnson, for instance, commenting ruefully that he was probably seen by the kids as 'a soft touch'. Yet Len also noted the opposite demand:

> I go away quite frequently with the bushwalkers; we just went out at Easter time, and they talked about the teachers. The teacher to them is—the good teacher is the guy that clobbers them, not physically, but stands on them and keeps them up to the mark. They were the less academically-capable kids, and they see education as being an achievement of qualifications, their Matriculation and School Certificate. That's what they see their education as, and the good teacher is the one who makes them get it; makes himself a pig, really.

What is striking here is that this is the view of kids in the lower streams, not just the 'academic achievers'. On our evidence, Len is right. The kids we talked to, by and large, did not want the teachers to relax control completely, and did want direction and help. Yet the fact of widespread resistance remains.

The pressure from parents, too, can be contradictory. There are many families where the school is seen as lax on discipline, the kids getting away with murder, and the teachers as letting the side down. The home tries to maintain 'standards', the school swims with the tide. Yet in many other families the parents, looking back on the brutality and indifference handed out by schools in their own childhoods, welcome the more relaxed and humane treatment their children are getting from teachers now. And some teachers feel that the discipline problems of the schools are exacerbated by the more authoritarian parents. Arlette Anderson thinks this, and gives chapter and verse. A Year 8 girl was acting up in class, and Arlette said to her that she wouldn't do this to her mother. Answer: 'Oh Christ no, my Dad would smash me one'. In another Year 8 class, doing a family role-playing exercise, the girl who was playing the mother began abusing and beating up the daughter; Arlette was appalled, but another person in the class explained, laughing, that the girl was just acting like her own mother. On this argument, the kids behave shockingly at school because they are taking out their frustrations and angers on the teachers.

The balance among these different pressures will vary from place to place, but the central fact is that in most cases the teachers are facing contradictory pressures and contradictory demands. This gives them a range of possible practices to choose from. This range varies from school to school so that what appears progressive in one context may be rather conventional in another. New teachers draw from the repertory offered by their current school.

The fact of contradiction also shapes the choice to be made. In particular, it shapes choice about discipline as one between laxity and firmness, being easy-going or being authoritatian, as a general style of management in the classroom and in other settings around the school. Position on this spectrum becomes an important part of a teacher's self-image. Doris Willoughby, for instance, repeatedly opened conversations by insisting 'I don't have any discipline problems'. That was the first and most important battle for her; she won it, and can now handle anything.

> One of the Matrics in the class finally got around to telling me that he thought I was a battle-axe. So that's probably about the right word for it. But now that he knows me at that level it's a different kettle of fish. Another one in the same class said: 'I can remember you had us for the first four weeks in First Year. You frightened the daylights out of us'.

Other teachers push as far as they reasonably can in the other direction. Joe Milwell tells this tale of playground duty:

> We get our pot smokers here at the school. We had a group of them last year. Used to get out on the cricket pitch and not worry anybody else. Smoke their pot, go to sleep in the afternoon lesson. They didn't worry anybody. They just enjoyed themselves. My only interest was to stop them smoking, because the rules of the school say kids don't smoke on the place. You stop them whenever you see them. I used to drift out there on the cricket pitch and you couldn't find a cigarette on them, and you're not going to press the Education Act to the stage where you get the kid to throw out his pockets. You've got the right under the Education Act to do it, but you're pushing things a bit hard if you try it. Anyway, they were putting their butts down under the tap plates of the watering sprinklers. It took nine months of duty out there to work out what was happening to the cigarette butts. If you'd sat up there with a

pair of binoculars on the top floor you'd have found out in five minutes.

There are differences of attitude here; but more importantly there is a range of *practices*, which not only differ from each other but actively interfere with each other. Doris and Joe teach in the same school. When Doris 'frightens the daylights' out of the kids, she is making it more difficult for Joe to construct the person-to-person, rather adult, take-responsibility-for-yourself kind of relationship with them that his teaching needs. When Joe lets the kids notionally conform to school rules, or go to sleep at the back of the class if they want to, he makes it harder for Doris to run the taut, teacher-centred classroom her teaching depends on.

This clash of strategies was plainly one of the most divisive and intractable issues among the staff of these schools. There are so many teachers, as Arlette Anderson remarks, that you cannot 'control' them all, i.e. pull them into line to present a united front to the kids.

> You're trying to be really strict with them, and they say, 'Oh Mrs Such-and-such says we can do that'. That's where it all breaks down.

The issue is particularly sticky where the division is not just between the individual teachers, but between whole departments.

Yet it has to be managed; and the schools have evolved mechanisms for doing so. One is to make discipline in general the responsibility of a particular senior member of staff, traditionally a deputy principal. The 'iron man' deputy who plays this role and is heavily depended on by the teachers is a familiar figure. One, by the name of Jones, was pungently contrasted with an over-liberal principal:

> Kids who perform outrageously in class, they can hurl furniture or abuse, to the nth degree, and if you go to the Boss, the Boss will tell them they're a naughty person. They might get a day's suspension. Jonesie will crucify them.

But Jonesie cannot stay for ever; indeed he did not, and the replacement was a man of a different stamp:

> This very strong deputy channelled everything through himself, and people got into the habit of sending discipline problems to him.

> This new guy, you'd be a fool to send anyone to him, you really would, because he sides with the kid.

The change of regime here is symbolic. This way of managing the discipline issue seems to have been getting less effective. Increasing opposition to corporal punishment has made the stock-in-trade of the tough deputy, the short sharp shock of the cane, less acceptable. More discipline issues now involve girls, who by law cannot be caned. Broadly, more emphasis is now being placed on discussion among the staff at large, and attempts to work out formal 'discipline policy' across the whole school. The problems and possibilities are explored by Hawkins in *Resistances to School*.

Our material suggests two general points about the question of discipline. Though nostalgic appeals to the 'better discipline in the past' imply that discipline is always the same thing, and schools just have more or less of it, this is not so. 'Discipline' is not a thing, it is a state of play in a very complex set of relationships between schools and their clienteles, teachers and students, administrators and teachers.

Some of these relationships are class relationships. It is a familiar fact that teachers find discipline issues harder to handle in schools with working-class clienteles than schools drawing from more affluent groups. Finer details may also be important. One of the schools in our study was having something of a discipline crisis because its catchment had been changed and now drew in more kids from the poorest and newly-immigrant parts of the working class.

Some of these relationships, also, are gender relationships. As noted above (p. 84), a rising tide of 'problems involving girls' has forced one school administration to make Margaret Atwill its trouble-shooter in this area. Len Johnson (p. 83) is condemned to lower-stream teaching because he is big and a man, and women are not thought able to control those classes. Faye Taylor notes how this interacts with patterns of adolescent growth. As the boys get large and 'elephant around' in Years 10 and 11, it requires considerable moral force on the part of women teachers to understand and manage them,

> because at that stage, you always have personality problems, and problems of physical size fitting them into the classroom, and

problems of getting them to start thinking on their own rather than
following a set pattern. It's all complicated with growing up.

And there are great differences in the rates of growth, to
complicate it further.

While 'growing up' may be a constant, the way it is done, and
the circumstances in which it is done, are certainly not. It is a
basic fact about class relations and gender relations that they
change historically. The school as an institution changes, as does
its clientele. So the terms in which 'discipline' issues have to be
posed and resolved must also change with time. And many
teachers are well aware of this. They know that, as with teaching
technique, tried and true methods that have worked in the past
will not keep on working now.

The second general point is that issues of 'discipline' cannot be
separated too sharply from issues of pedagogy. Keeping control
in the classroom is certainly an essential teaching skill, but
teachers have to be very demoralised before they are keeping
control merely for the sake of keeping control. Most teachers
want the kids to *learn*; control is a prerequisite for this. Lack of
control is experienced as an obstacle to the teacher's more
serious work. I have quoted an eloquent statement of this from
Rosa Marshall: 'you were...trying to mould them into some sort
of social being rather than teaching a subject'. (p. 51).

Frustration on this score is easily built up, and can motivate
an interest in drastic solutions, such as Rosa's abandoning ship
altogether, or other teachers' support for the cane. It is at first
surprising to find a modernist like Andrew Sutting, the computer
expert, supporting the cane. He gives an uncharacteristically
muddled set of reasons:

> If it's got to be done, it's got to be done and that's it. Afterwards
> you forget about it, so does the kid probably. If it has achieved
> the purpose that's that, that's the way it should be done. It's got a
> place in—I can't see how it is ever going to really drop out, in
> school. It has got to be there, otherwise it would be chaos. As
> much as people say it shouldn't be there, their arguments are too
> airy-fairy. What are they going to replace it with? I don't know.

What comes through in such moments is the tone more than the
argument: the yearning for a quick, once-and-for-all solution
that will let the teachers get on with their Proper Business.

'Discipline' is an extremely important theme in the public

image of private schooling. It means many things. Discipline is the production of a particular personal style that will ease entry into appropriate social networks. Paul O'Neill, a private school old boy himself, notes wryly of the school he is teaching in now:

> Employers say for example, 'Oh, you went to Milton'. And Milton College has a name for short hair and kids that are conformist. So people hope they would be able to get a decent amount of work out of them, and so on.

Discipline is a guarantee to the parents that the kids will not get into trouble: that there will be no drugs at the school, little physical violence (except on the football field), and—an important though usually tacit underpinning of segregated girls' private schools—no pregnancies. Discipline is a guarantee that the kids will be kept at work, not allowed to slacken off, and will therefore maximise their chances of access to university via the certifying public exams. Discipline is a guarantee that the kids will show due respect for adults, will not turn into juvenile delinquents, will not talk an unintelligible dialect, will not wear outrageous clothes, or dye their hair, or listen only to the music of raucous and ill-mannered rock stars. In such ways, the school's claim to maintain discipline is an answer to parents' fears. It is important to the private schools that such fears should remain lively ones among their potential customers.

In *Making the Difference* we gave too smooth an account of the 'good order' of the elite private schools. The description was correct, but we did not give enough recognition to the reasons why the good order was important, the energy that went into producing it, or the strategies by which the private schools tried to achieve it. These schools have their discipline problems too. Glen Moncrieff remarks of St Paul's College:

> I don't like rigid discipline, but I *deplore* the lack of respect that I see in this place, for teachers.

Other teachers mentioned unrest in classrooms, indifference to school work, swearing, shoplifting, smoking pot, and sometimes mass outbursts against discipline, among the ills that private schools are heir to. The list is not so very different from what goes on in the state schools; this is resistance from the kids, and their means of resistance are much the same.

Some of the techniques used by the teachers, also, are much

the same. Heavy-handed classroom authority is one; the most emphatic endorsements of the scare-them-first-and-relax-later approach that we heard came from private school teachers. The kids sometimes get yelled at and abused. One teacher we interviewed in a private school has decided not to send a child to this particular school, because

> I wouldn't like any child of mine to be spoken to in the way that the head speaks to the kids.

Corporal punishment is not only allowed, it is ritualised, in the boys' schools. And as in the state schools, effort has to be put into co-ordinating the teachers' practices. Two of the independent schools we studied had recently had staff conferences on discipline policy. Every so often there is a blitz on discipline—uniform, punctuality, or such like—and it is the teachers who have to enforce it. Sometimes it backfires. At one school there was a blitz on punctuality (students getting to classes exactly on time) which was much resented by the kids. One form turned it on its head, openly criticised teachers for being late, locked the door if the teacher was not on time, and called out:

> That's ten minutes of our fees you owe us.

The discipline campaign, in short, was undermining the authority of the teachers. The school had to back off.

Where the private schools we studied differ significantly from the working–class schools is in the persistence and intensity with which these disciplinary techniques are used. Rules of behaviour, dress and speech are woven together with less formal but equally insistent models of acceptable personal style, into a regime of controls that extend not only into the peer-group life of the kids at school but also outside the school.

Further, an apparatus of surveillance, reporting, and correction is built up to monitor the kids' compliance with this regime. In classic fashion the older students are recruited to police the younger, as 'prefects'; but once again the main weight falls on the teachers. When a private school gets slack, it is likely to be because this surveillance and correction has ceased to work. When a slack school is renovated by a new principal, beefing up this side of the staff's effort is likely to be an important part of the strategy. It had certainly been so in three of the schools we studied. What might be called preventative discipline is an im-

portant side of the personal contact with students which is
stressed in the private schools' public relations.

Here is an example of how elaborate such regimes of contact
and control can be, with careful provision for back-up in case
the first-line provision breaks down:

> I think the system if it's followed through as outlined by the
> school is very good. For instance we're supposed to be the kind of
> people that the kids won't have any hesitation in coming to if he's
> got problems. If he won't come to the housemaster he'll go to one
> of the teachers associated with the houses, there's usually two or
> three tutors associated with the house. Sometimes, let's put it this
> way, there might be a block in relations with the housemaster, you
> can't help this, so the kids are then encouraged to go to the tutor.
> And I think the fact that every boy in this school is known fairly
> well by some member of staff, it's a *very* important thing. You
> don't get the anonymity that you get in some of the very big
> schools. You know and I know that we've got state schools where
> there are two and a half thousand kids. Well is every kid in that
> school known by some member of staff, I wonder? That's not the
> case here. Every child is known by some member of staff; some of
> them are known by many members of staff (laugh) in more ways
> than one (another laugh).

With kids who go beyond low-level resistance to this regime
the private schools have another resort. They can throw them
out. John Welton describes how the drug problem was handled
at a boys' school he used to teach at:

> It was very clean, and it was clean because I think two things. The
> headmaster has a [belief] there that the less these things are talked
> about, the less boys will be thinking about it. So there was never
> allowed any discussion on drugs; and he never allowed the drug
> referral people or anybody like that ever to come into the school.
> And he never spoke about it to the boys. He would speak to
> parents. And the second thing was that within ten minutes, I'm
> sure that was all it was, when those boys were discovered they were
> out of the school. It was very very quick. And he never made any
> announcements, but it was known. That flies in the face of the
> modern thought on it, but that's how he handled it. And he was
> able to say, well, he'd been here for eighteen years and his school
> was not troubled.

Those expelled kids no doubt landed in the state school down the
road; and no doubt their places were taken by the children of

parents worried about the decline of discipline in the state schools... If a private school does this too often its reputation will suffer, but provided its market position is good, the device of expelling trouble is effective just as a threat.

There are, then, strong pressures for conformity on the kids, and as will be argued in chapter 9, on the teachers too. This certainly makes it easier to keep order. But it is not necessarily in the best interest of the ruling class that their rising generation grow up unable to see beyond the ends of their noses. More immediately, while some teachers embrace a strong disciplinary regime with enthusiasm, the more professionalised teachers are likely to experience it as a stifling conservatism, and may not care to stay in it. Too much disciplinary pressure, and the school may suffer academically by losing its best teachers. Alternatively, teachers may turn against the regime. Some refuse to enforce rules they regard as ridiculous. One even expressed regret at having inadvertently caused the expulsion of a boy for smoking pot.

In all of this the school's market position is a key consideration; and that leads to a final point of difference from the state schools. To the private schools as institutions the *appearance* of discipline is as important as the reality. The rigid rules about uniform dress are precisely about keeping the school's public face burnished. At one of the schools we studied the kids started using back packs instead of cases. The school quickly moved to incorporate this fashion into the uniform, and have now got a manufacturer selling 'school approved' back packs to the kids.

At a more serious level, the most striking thing about the drugs story quoted above is not so much the speed of the expulsion, as the headmaster's elaborate information-management. Who was told what was most carefully controlled, so at the end '*he was able to say*, well, he'd been here for eighteen years and his school was not troubled'. Other teachers too commented on the importance of what is and is not talked about, sex and drugs being high on the list for silence. For instance, one of the men noted the general embarrassment in his school on the subject of sex education. The Chaplain used to give moralistic lectures, which were not terribly successful; then the Family Life Movement was brought in, which worked so far as the boys were concerned, but it was held to be indecorous to have a woman doing the talking about sex; so now 'I think the headmaster gives some chat, but I'm not exactly sure about that'. The less said, the better.

The circumstances of private schooling shape discipline issues for teachers in a rather different way from the situation in working-class state schools. They rarely, if ever, have to do the gut-wrenching lion-tamer act that public school teachers, especially in lower-stream classes, often have to do. As we showed in *Making the Difference* a degree of compliance by the kids is a given, so discipline is rarely a question of sheer survival as a teacher. On the other hand, to sustain this situation teachers are under pressure to participate in a much finer-meshed network of surveillance and regulation. They may find this distasteful or even repugnant to their professionalism. To put it in a phrase, the central issue in the one case is survival, with the pressure coming from below; in the other conformity, with the pressure coming from above.

Teaching and the emotions

Margaret Blackall remarks about being a teacher (p. 20):

> My husband is not part of this life. He has nothing to do with teaching ... He doesn't know the pressures.

To people outside teaching, both the strong personal involvement ('part of this life'), and the idea of 'pressure', may seem strange. School teaching is by common repute an easy job, a 'soft cop' with short hours, long holidays, and little physical exertion. Conservative politicians and right-wing professors of philosophy can rely on having an audience whenever they get an uncontrollable urge to do some teacher-bashing.

What Margaret Blackall says, nevertheless, is valid. Len Johnson, a teacher of a very different style but equally dedicated to his trade, and more experienced, remarks:

> I run my health right down every year. I lost two hundred bucks when I came off school last week. You know, bronchitis.

Teachers who take their job seriously do get exhausted by the end of each school year. The 'pressure' is real, and it has an impact on one's physical health, mood, personal relationships and sense of self. Lorraine Smart:

Do you like your job?

Yes, I do. I find it a big strain.

What is it about it that's a strain?

I find the psychological and even physical confrontation with kids constantly. In the first year of teaching, the strain is immense. If you care at all about what you're doing, the strain is immense. And I truly felt at one stage at least during last year that I was really going insane. I mean that quite seriously. I was losing my sense of judgement. Little trying incidents became terrible catastrophes. I really was beginning to go off the rails emotionally. I would feel like bursting into tears at the drop of a hat.

Teaching may be physically one of the soft jobs; but in terms of *emotional* pressure, it is one of the most demanding.

To understanding high school teachers and their work it is important to register the emotional texture of the relationships they have with changing, growing, sometimes tense and mistrustful, adolescents. In our interviews this came out most clearly when teachers were discussing particular kids. Here is an example from Mary Coleman, a young teacher at Greenway High:

Andrew and another kid, Benny, sat together last year, and sat together this year when Andrew was here. They're both big physically, and perhaps they think they're more mature because they're big. But at the beginning of the year, he and Benny tended to be—not a discipline problem, but they tended to be, I felt, antagonistic. Last year they were a bit painful, possibly because they thought they were more mature, I don't know. But as the year progressed, I felt that we got on a lot better. Either they accepted me more, or they matured more, I don't know. And I found that in History, Andrew was interested in discussions, was very interested, very aware, fairly good general knowledge and interested in politics and things. So I found that he'd always take part in discussions when he was there, make intelligent comments, argue and so on.

Multiply that by 100 or 150, with some relationships worsening while others improve and others reach impasse; flavour with the odd confrontation, teenage crush, flood of laughter and burst of tears; stir in relationships with the colleagues in the staffroom; and you have some idea of the complexity of the emotional currents flowing through one teacher's week at work.

And that is only at the one-to-one level. Teachers' work is mainly organised in terms of classes; and each class has a distinctive character, which reacts back on the teachers' emotions. To continue with Mary Coleman, she tells of one class that gave her a real lift:

What sort of approach do you usually use?
It depends on the class. The class I had this year as I said were usually very bright, so I found that we could do set novels with them, in a fair amount of depth, and they'd be able to write intelligently on them. Poetry I did, and they didn't like, they all complained and moaned about it. When I tried some bits of it they'd like, but even with poetry they could write fairly well on, and I did a lot of plays and drama and speeches and things, because they were that sort of class. And we had a lot of real extraverts in it that could do some really funny stuff. But I tried it with my second years this year, and they were a bright class too, but they just didn't seem to be the same sort of extraverted types that that sort of thing went well with. It was really strange. So that class were always saying 'Can't we do more plays?', 'Can't we do more speeches?', and I'd say 'Well we've got to do some serious work'. So we'd do two weeks of serious work, then we'd spend a few lessons rabbling around doing plays and stuff. They were really great.

But then:

I wouldn't teach social science and English if I didn't like them. It depends though, on the classes you get. This year the two third-year classes I had were tremendous, really good classes, we got on really well. They were great kids, we did a lot of work. I had an absolutely rotten second year class, which has really put me off teaching second year history forever!

And of course you cannot tell, from one year to the next, which you are going to get.

The teacher's relationships with kids, then, are emotionally demanding at several levels. Yet even that has not quite got to the heart of the matter. In these passages Mary Coleman is not reporting on an incidental aspect of her work, or on some emotional preconditions, hurdles she has to jump before she can get on with her teaching. She is inside these relationships *as a teacher*. In a real sense these emotional relationships *are* her work, and managing them is a large part of her labour process. Keeping order, and getting the kids to learn, both require operating on the emotions of the kids through the emotions of the teacher.

A beginning teacher, facing the problem of keeping order, lives on her nerves until she has worked out a strategy of survival. Lorraine Smart, describing how she was 'beginning to go off the rails', suggests how stressful that is. A more experienced teacher is likely to be less vulnerable, but is not therefore less involved. For whatever strategy of control is adopted always requires an emotional commitment in a particular direction. By pursuing a particular strategy one becomes a particular kind of teacher and a particular kind of person.

With some teachers the commitment becomes so routine that person and strategy grow together, so to speak; and in meeting them one is hardly conscious of the join, merely of an established persona. The fact that there is an emotional commitment within a strategy of control becomes much more apparent when it is under stress. Arlette Anderson explodes:

> They make me feel like a terribly old-fashioned strait-laced woman, while I'm here. I really get that whole blast of the middle-class schoolteacher trying to impress her morals upon the students. And then I turn round and say to myself 'Well are my morals so bloody bad?' I'm not about to change.

Joe Guaraldi, equally frustrated, notes how the 'authoritarianism' of the control strategies of the school (p. 104) erodes the mutual respect between teachers and pupils that he would be comfortable with:

> The kids tend to have this attitude here that teachers are something that crawl under the woodwork at 5 o'clock and emerge at 9 o'clock in the morning to teach them for a day. It's very unrealistic, and that's one of the reasons why kids tend to rebel against teachers, is that they don't regard them as human beings. They regard them as some sort of automaton that's just there to teach.

And he also notes one of the reasons for it—the pressure teachers are under from other teachers to get on top of their classes and stay there.

> It's just the role that the teacher is expected to have in a school like this. Here, you come in, and if you're not a person who's going to have absolutely quiet classes, you're made to feel like an idiot if your classes aren't absolutely quiet. Because people will come by and...people like Peter Jones [the previous deputy] will

come and peer in at your windows and make sure your class is
absolutely quiet, you know. You're made to feel like a bit of a
fool if your class is a bit noisier than all the others.

Teasing the threads out, we may say that there are three
aspects of teachers' emotional involvement in control. First, the
emotional pressures that push the teacher towards a strategy of
control (Lorraine Smart's 'terrible catastrophes', Joe Guaraldi's
'feeling like an idiot'). Second, the emotional aspect of the
exercise of control; both from moment to moment (giving
orders, praise, sarcasm; asking, pleading, shouting; facing kids
down in direct clashes, or dodging the issue and sending them to
the deputy) and over the longer term (Rosa Marshall's dilemma
about taking moral responsibility for what kind of people the
kids become, p. 51). Third, the emotional consequences of a
particular practice of teaching: the kind of person one is
becoming, or has become (Arlette Anderson's middle-class
moralist).

Teachers become the kind of people they are, partly because
they participate year in and year out in a school system of a
particular kind. They do not necessarily take on the colouring of
the system, as they may pit themselves against it or try to
manoeuvre around it; but it still leaves its mark. Such disciplinary facts about the system as its hierarchical management
and control over teachers, its history of violence against children
(until recently a career teacher would routinely have hit hundreds
of children in the course of duty, sometimes with a cane and
sometimes without), and the levels of physical and emotional
frustration it requires masses of kids to endure (again as a matter
of routine), must have long-term effects on the social character
of teachers. We met some, well on in their careers, who did seem
tired and blunted people. It seemed likely that this dimension of
schooling had helped to make them that way.

Less conspicuous than the dramas of resistance and control,
but at least as important, is the emotional dimension of
'teaching' in the narrower sense of getting the kids to learn.

Rosa Marshall remarked (p. 51) on her need for the kids to
like her; this is not a neurotic need for affection, it is a simple
fact that her successful pedagogy depends on this. Phyllis Howell
remarked (p. 69) on the need for teachers to like the kids. That

is not universally true, but it is common enough. We listened to hundreds of descriptions of pupils by their teachers, and while few were exactly star-struck, a great many were affectionate. Theo Georges:

I like the lad a lot. Oh yeah, I reckon he's terrific! I really enjoy his company. He's a pleasant lad, I always have a laugh with him, and he always says he's going to try and do things, but he never does. He never reaches the final thing. But he's—I enjoy his company in class.

Even where there has been real strife, there will usually be pleasure in re-establishing good personal relationships. Joe Guaraldi:

Yes, she'll sort of, well, walk into the class and say 'G'day Mr Geronimo' and stuff like this, in a sort of stirry sense. And some of the kids get a bit jacked off eventually with that sort of loud-mouth stuff. But I got on very well with her this year actually. I was one of her favourite teachers. Just a sort of clash of personalities last year. I called her a bitch at one stage! She got very upset and decided that I couldn't call her that, and decided to stomp off on me. I think she decided that she was going to be out to get me this year, but I got onto her good side, and we got on very well.

This willingness to like the kids, even when they are not 'doing well' or 'doing what they are told', is an important fact about teachers' work. The schools would be very much more tense and alienating places if it were not the case.

Yet liking the kids has its own dangers for the craft of teaching. Joe Milwell thoughtfully observes of the 'more popular teachers':

They live for that class and they take that class...that kid's interests to heart, and they identify with them, and the kids identify with them.

It is familiar that kids in schools often identify with a favourite teacher; the reverse also happens. In particular it takes the form of the teacher taking responsibility for the kids' learning. Margaret Blackall's description of a class that has 'taken advantage' of her (p. 16) is a good example—*they* slack off on the homework and

I get very frustrated.

She has taken on the students' problems as her own; and the

emotional tangle that results is evident, as she makes the students feel guilty because she has got angry because they have let her down...

Emotional involvement with the kids' success in learning is hard to avoid. It is part of caring for kids, which is an important thing with teachers. Margaret Blackall's unexpected opposition to streaming (chapter 1) is motivated by her capacity to care about what the school is doing to those 'untalented' first-year kids being streamed down. Jack Ryan's whole pedagogy (chapter 5) centres on his capacity to care about the same unprepossessing bunch. Almost all the teachers I have mentioned in this section are from the state schools, so it is appropriate to add Glen Moncrieff's story about a bottom-stream class in the boys' private school where he works. They were going on an overnight excursion:

> One of them, who's sixteen stone and big and ungainly and very low intelligence, came up to me with a programme and said, 'My *name's* in this programme'. And I said 'Yes'. He said 'But look, my name is here'. And he said 'I've never had my name on anything in my whole time at this school. Can I have this and show it to Mum and Dad?' Well, I learnt a hell of a lot from that.

Teachers' willingness to care about kids is one of the nicest things about them. It is one of the most important, though least tangible, assets that the education system has. Some teachers get it burnt out of them, and become indifferent or injured. Some are no doubt authoritarian from the start, some go into the job for the money or to get a higher education. But for the majority of teachers we interviewed, this capacity to care is a fact and a real presence in their work.

It can lead to over-involvement. It can lock teachers in to situations they might be better out of, attempts they might be better off not making. It can make *failure* of the teaching effort a personally devastating event. Many of the problems of emotional involvement are visible enough to teachers. In *Making the Difference* we suggested briefly that 'teaching is an emotionally-dangerous occupation' and that the reaction of most teachers was to withdraw, to keep their distance. This was an overstatement, but it is certainly true that a degree of withdrawal, a conscious containment of the impact, is an important option for teachers and one which many take. Len Johnson made his observation on how teaching affects his health (p. 115) in the middle of a discussion of how other teachers do otherwise:

> It's still very much a traditionally oriented school. The teacher considers that this job is done in the classroom, and then they nick off home. And you can't really blame them because, you know, I run my health right down every year [etc]. Practicality is the whole thing. And there's a lot of people who've been around long enough to know that you don't take on more than you ought to. I tend to be a mug in that respect.

The strategy of limiting emotional involvement is not necessarily a sign of indifference or mediocrity as a teacher. Alison Chant, a stunningly successful and highly professional teacher, insists that she is here to 'teach' them, not 'love' them. Information and understanding are what is useful to them; and anyway how can you love a bunch of kids in a classroom? Glen Moncrieff, who told the story about the boy with his name in the programme, also told about another boy:

> He's got family problems, in the sense that his mother literally doesn't like him, and is honest enough to say so.
> *Why*?
> Well, she doesn't. It's a sort of delicate area. If a mother says she doesn't like her son, you don't really like to probe too much. I'm not very good at probing like that. I could probably guess...

In short, he does not want to know; there are worms best left in the can.

On the other hand there are teachers like Sheila Goffman (chapter 1) and Rosa Marshall (chapter 4) whose reaction to the pressures is enthusiastic engagement, using the full spectrum of their own emotional responses (and the kids') as tools in their teaching. In such circumstances, teaching, far from being an emotionally dangerous occupation, can be a thoroughly supportive one. Phyllis Howell, deputy head at St Margaret's, is one example of how a whole pattern of life can be constructed in and around teaching, in a way that is emotionally secure and satisfying. She relates well to the kids and to the staff. Her classroom practices have been worked out, are obviously succeeding, and need only fine-tuning. She gets immense satisfaction from enlightening the kids, broadening their outlooks, and setting them on the path towards the professions.

Not all teachers can be arranged on a dimension from involvement to non-involvement. Joe Milwell, the author of some of

our most quotable quotes, came to teaching after a number of
years in business. At times his relationships with kids sound like
scenes from Rudyard Kipling:

> Never had a brush with him in two years. If he at times over-
> stepped the mark, got a bit cheeky, I only had to point out to him
> that he was out of order and he apologised. Came to heel straight
> away. Proper good lad, always has been.

and

> Very fair-minded lad. Good character right through. Good stern
> stuff.

Joe is no blushing innocent about teaching as a trade—he
supports his union firmly, and is clear about the need for
control, especially in the rougher classes. He says that he likes 'a
bit of distance in a relationship'. Yet he, in a fuller sense than
most other teachers, has *chosen* to teach, and thinks of himself
as a committed professional. He works very hard—60 or 70
hours a week, he says, and that is believable—knows the kids
individually, finds out what he can about their family background, and so on. He describes his classroom:

> I try to do a lot more for my class, just quietly, without any
> drum-beating and flag-waving... You can tell which is my class by
> walking around, with the damage to the lockers [in other rooms].
> Even if you didn't know that, you can look for the one that's got
> posters in it... They've got pride in their classroom.

What he seems to be doing is constructing a relationship with the
kids based not on taking responsibility for them, but on a
genuine if under-stated respect for them. He expects them to
take responsibility for themselves. If they do, all praise; if they
do not, they have to wear the consequences. In effect, he says to
the kids, you do your job and I'll do mine. He offers them a
'fair deal' (his own phrase), and sees to it that he keeps his end
of the bargain.

I suspect a pattern like this is more generally useful as a model
for good practice than that of Sheila Goffman or Phyllis Howell.
It is probably more sustainable for most teachers over the long
run, and it gives a bit more space for critical reflection on what
one is doing. At the same time, it would be wrong to imply that
there can be only one model of good practice. While teachers'
strategies sometimes interfere with each other, they also draw on

each other, and arguments stimulate new developments. There is room for a range of practice in any lively school.

Looking more broadly at working-class schooling, it is clear that a major part of the teachers' experience is the fact of massive failure. Most of the kids do not stay the full high school course; and while they are there, do not show great enthusiasm for what the teachers have to offer; and especially the knowledge, embodied in the academic curriculum, that teachers collectively value most. Given the tendency for teachers to take responsibility for the kids' learning, this collective failure to learn is a heavy structural pressure on teachers' self-esteem, resilience, and enthusiasm for their job.

A number of teachers felt that teaching had got tougher in the course of time. Margaret Atwill for instance, thinking about a career that goes back to the 1940s, put it this way:

Do you like teaching?
Yes. At one time I would have said it without any hesitation at all. I don't think I enjoy it quite as much now; although I still enjoy being in the classroom more than the other sorts of jobs.
What made the difference in your attitude?
To teaching? I think it's become more of a strain and more difficult.
Why's that?
I think partly because of the greater variety of students coming into the high schools. At one time it was probably more clear cut, the accepted course and that sort of thing were more clear cut. I think most of the students were interested in doing well, whereas I don't think that's true now. We have got a lot of students in high school who are not very interested in doing well. I think, for instance, back in the time when I was teaching in the country, because of the type of children who were coming on to high school, you thought you were doing something for them. You were giving them what they wanted, therefore it was satisfying to do this. And I think now there are all these doubts raised as to what should we be giving the students; and this great variety of students that come on to high school. One wonders just what it is that they look for in high school. And because of all these doubts being raised, and because you've got a big class, so many of whom are not interested and who therefore often do resent the teacher, it's more difficult. Age might come into it, too, of course. You get slower; and I think that's probably true, I think I've got a bit slower.

This is an interesting passage, most of all for Margaret's clear sense of larger social changes funnelling in to the high school and reconstructing relationships there, in particular making it more difficult for the teachers to operate and to get satisfaction in their job. The shift away from regular formal examinations has had a similar effect. Faye Taylor, for instance, notes how the main motivation for learning used to be a 'blackmail of tests'. Now if the teachers are to get results they have to find their own ways of making the kids interested in learning. Again, more pressure on the teachers' skills, more risk to their self-esteem.

Such material offers glimpses of the inner history of teaching, not detailed enough for certainty but rich enough to show that there have been transformations going on, and to suggest some of their directions. It seems a reasonable hypothesis that teaching in the public system over the past few decades has become more demanding, in the sense of being more complex, more open-ended, and placing more responsibility on the individual teacher and the immediate work group. It also seems likely that the shape of the pressures on teachers has changed, from a situation where the main pressure came from an extremely hierarchical management, to one where the main pressure comes from a much more varied and much less submissive clientele.

The joy of teaching

Talking of pressure, control, difficulty and responsibility is inevitable, but there is also a brighter colour in teachers' relationships with kids. Part of the emotional pattern of teaching is pleasure.

Glen Moncrieff started teaching more or less by accident. He needed a wage, his old school was short of teachers, and he asked the head for a job:

I was quite honest about the fact that it wasn't my future
vocation. And in a month, I decided, that was it. Brother, there
wasn't anything that was going to drag me away from teaching.

When Glen talks about his teaching it is very obvious that he enjoys it. He likes the personal relationships, he likes the professional challenge, he gets a kick out of his successes with slow learners, he finds teaching is opening doors for him, and his career is taking off.

Many others talk about the pleasures of teaching. Some of these discussions have to do with what the job has allowed teachers to do with their lives. Alison Chant was a housewife until the age of 45, and 'by that time I was just about flattened', with no self-image, completely absorbed in family and children. Going teaching allowed her to reconstitute herself as a person with an independent reality, in other people's eyes and in her own. Roy Clive's needs are simpler. He was a state representative footballer. He likes teaching because it allows him to play lots of football.

Every so often, teaching yields high points, moments of keen pleasure. Phyllis Howell mentions an unexpected one. The day before our interview she was handed, by a non-academic 'immature' student, an unsolicited essay in her subject. Alex Stimson mentions an expected one. For the last four years, he has got a 100 per cent pass rate for his students in the Matriculation maths exams.

For some teachers the pleasures of teaching centre on the human relations involved. We have quoted teachers talking about their liking for kids, about enjoying their company and having a laugh together. For some teachers, like Sheila Goffman in chapter 1, human relations are themselves a fine art.

For others, the development of their professional sophistication and skill as an instructor is the main source of satisfaction. The discussion of the labour process in chapter 6 suggested that these skills can become very refined and elaborate indeed. Teachers like Alison Chant and Bettina Alt take an intellectual pleasure in solving the more recondite problems of their trade.

And with some, the human relations and the exercise of the trade are indistinguishable. Theo Georges:

> I love tech studies, I love doing it. I love being creative with my hands. And I also wanted to be a teacher because I love being with people, working with them, and sharing what I have.

Finally—and perhaps closest to the heart of the mystery—is the alchemy of the classroom. I have quoted Mary Coleman (p. 117) on the class that came alive and the one that did not. She cannot explain it. For all the research and talk about schools, getting people to learn remains something of a mystery. It is certainly an extraordinarily complex business, an interplay of intellectual, emotional, and social processes so intricate that it virtually defies analysis. A great deal of what teachers actually do in their time on the classroom floor is based on intuitive knowledge and instant reactions, not on formal plans. And when you get it right, when it does work really well, it is a most exhilarating experience. People who have not taught can have little idea of what it is like to have *taught well*, to be buoyed up and swept along by the response of students who are really learning. One reaches for metaphors: chemical reactions, currents, setting alight, taking fire. But however difficult to describe, let alone explain, the experience is a real one, and it is something that most teachers, in whatever part of the education system, have at least some of the time.

Summary, chapter 8

Teaching depends on being able to control the kids. What seems a simple task is actually an extremely complex set of relationships involving gender, class and age, and working through pedagogy as well as policing. An antagonism is built into the structure of mass schooling; difficulties are compounded by contradictory demands from kids and from parents. Teachers have evolved a range of strategies for handling discipline, which often cut across each other. School-wide strategies are evolved but are impossible to make consistent. The elite private schools put a great deal of energy into maintaining a tighter disciplinary regime; their teachers have to police this, not always willingly. Teaching is an emotionally demanding job. Teachers necessarily work via their emotional relationships to individual pupils and whole classes. Maintaining control implies emotional strategies that form them as teachers and as people. Getting the kids to learn often means an identification with them, a willingness to care about them and commonly to like them. This risks over-involvement. Many teachers therefore restrict their commitment to the kids; some embrace it, while some work out a relationship based on mutual respect but not mutual identification. Teachers of working-class kids are under constant emotional pressure; it is likely that this has increased historically. Teaching can also be an exhilarating and joyful experience, expanding the teacher's life through skills or human relations, or both. Teaching well is a thrill.

9

The school as a workplace

Supervision and control

Social control in schools is usually discussed in terms of teachers' control of the kids. Like almost all workers, teachers themselves are subject to a system of supervision.

The pictures of this we were given by different teachers are curiously inconsistent. Some of them lay a great deal of stress on their freedom from control in ordinary classroom work. As Alan Watson puts it,

> In the classroom, you're very much left to your own devices. If you want to change something, you just go ahead and do it, simple as that.

For some, this sense of freedom is one of the great attractions of teaching. Others feel not only supervised, but positively invigilated. The subject senior insists on seeing their weekly class tests; the deputy stalks past the classroom and peers in at the window. They get 'jumped upon' if the subject senior doesn't like what they are doing, carpeted by the head if they lose control of their classes.

Both of these perceptions are sound. Given the labour process described in chapter 6, most teachers work most of the time in separate rooms where they cannot be seen, and with luck cannot be heard, by their fellow-workers or by management. They do not have a product that can be weighed, counted, or sampled for quality control. The technical characteristics of teachers' work thus make them impossible to supervise in the ways that are usual with other groups of workers.

Added to this, there are good reasons why school managers might prefer to minimise the supervision of classroom teachers. Supervision is costly, and there are always competing claims for resources. Close supervision causes resentment; it has been a fruitful source of industrial unrest in education as in other industries. And close supervision also contradicts the ideology of 'professionalism' which education authorities often want to encourage among teachers for other reasons. Professionals (supposedly) supervise themselves, governed by their technical knowledge and professional ethics. This notion has been an effective weapon in campaigns by teacher unions against management control, for instance against the powers of the inspectorate over individual teachers' careers.[5]

Yet it also matters to the authorities that teachers actually do what they are being paid to do, and a system of supervision has been constructed. Within the secondary school it has two tiers, heads of departments, and principals and deputies. How this system actually works, and what balance between the centripetal and centrifugal forces results, can vary a good deal. Where heads of department, deputies and principals wear their power lightly, the teachers may have almost complete autonomy on a day-to-day basis. In other situations the school authorities may intervene a great deal more. In schools undergoing renovation the intervention is likely to be extensive and sustained.

Broadly speaking, the authorities have reserve powers. Joe Guaraldi tells of a case where they were used, and he was kept on probation at a stage when teachers normally gain permanency:

> Well, I've had arguments with them [the senior staff] before. Like why we had to hand up our tests, every time we set a class test it's supposed to go back to them so they could check it, and their excuse supposedly is that they've got to learn from the sort of questions that we set our kids. They're fairly stupid things, but I had arguments and conflicts with them before. And one of them in particular whom I've had a few conflicts with carries a fair bit of weight. I didn't realise when I was doing these things and having the arguments that when my probationary point came up they would all be used against me in evidence, but they were. The deputy would bring up things like being late for lessons by a few minutes or something, and actually every trivial thing that I've done wrong in the school was brought up, and they decided that I was going to stay on probation.

That is unusual, but it can happen.

In the private schools the same sort of thing happens informally. Staff who are 'not of like mind', in Angus Barr's

genteel phrase (chapter 3), are quietly invited to pack their bags
and go. As with the kids, the ideological surveillance of teachers
is more insistent in the private schools than in the state system.
Julius Abernethy indicates the kind of thing involved, in explaining what the authorities at his school are looking for in a
teacher:

> I think it was more or less a personal example. Particularly looking
> for committed Christian professional staff. First and foremost was
> the academic qualification, but coupled with this was the general
> influence on the boys. They could look to this teacher and say,
> you know, he conducts himself in a proper Christian manner, if I
> can use that phrase. Not necessarily that the man would be
> committed as a Christian so much as he would be committed to
> Christian principles—there's a difference between the two as I'm
> sure you would appreciate. But the sort of thing—you don't have a
> fellow who perhaps *openly* advertises the fact that he's a
> homosexual, or promiscuous, or something like that, that the kids
> would know about.

Teachers in private schools are vulnerable to this kind of surveillance and control. They are less likely to have formal qualifications, especially formal teacher training, than state school
staff. Their unions are markedly weaker. Their contracts of
employment are less regularised. And their conditions are less
subject to public scrutiny, precisely because of the 'privacy' of
the schools. Though dissident staff like Rosa Marshall (chapter
4) exist in these schools, people as up-front about radical ideas
as she is are very much the exception. We also talked to teachers
in these schools who sat on their opinions in the staffroom,
and said nothing about their private lives, because they were
very scared of losing their jobs. They felt vulnerable, and were
intimidated.

The political order of the school

The supervision of teachers is part of a management effort to
produce a particular pattern of authority and accepted set of
practices in the school as a whole. While some teachers have
only a cloudy idea of how the school works as an institution,
others have it in very sharp focus. Faye Taylor, mathematics
teacher at Greenway High, has it laid out like a lesson in
algebra:

Can we come back to the school for a bit. How does it operate?
Well, it operates as a hierarchy of teachers: one headmaster, several
seniors, including deputy heads at that level. The seniors have their
apportioned areas, which is organised. They then are presented with
a mob of assistant teachers who perform whatever is asked of them
irrespective of training. The programme of work is issued, it is
generally carried out, but there is no actual check to see it has
been done so. So it relies on the conscience and stamina of the
individual teachers. The net result of the material presented in the
classroom is probably very variable. The students operate in class
units, doing more or less what they're told, with very little choice
as to what they would want to be doing. They have a choice of
subject in the senior school, but even so they don't really know
what they are choosing, so they blindly enter into a course. They
have a lot of enjoyment and fun with the other students in the
group, they generally play all the games which try to get out of
work, but they expect results so they're prepared to do some. So
we work basically on a co-operative system between student and
teacher, which is tied up with whether or not parents expect results,
or whether or not teacher forces results.

This set of connections may be called the *political order* of the
school: the pattern of authority and consent, alliance and co-
operation, resistance and opposition, that characterises the
institution as a whole. This pattern differs from school to
school, and changes over the years of a school's history. It is a
state of play, not a written constitution. It is influenced by the
patterns of power in the larger society, notably by the state of
class and gender relations, but is not rigidly determined from
outside. Local alliances, conflicts and initiatives affect the shape
those larger structures assume within the life of the school.

In every school we studied, the principal had markedly more
influence than anyone else; a headship means real power, though
never unchallenged power. In the state schools the principal's
authority is shared with a deputy, sometimes more than one, and
the style of administration depends a good deal on the relationship evolved. A familiar outcome is that they develop a good-
cop/bad-cop routine, with the principal providing the sympa-
thetic ear and the velvet glove, the deputy providing the iron fist.

The flavour of the process of management is nicely brought
out by Jack Ryan:

The Boss has progressive ideas in many ways that aren't popular
with a lot of people.

With the staff?

Yes. We have the usual division into conservative and progressive,
if you can use those labels. Probably 'traditional' better than
conservative. ...The big problem to me is assessment. We had a
preliminary enquiry, we found we've got anomalies, and the Boss
said it was so hot we'd better shelve it. I said that was his
approach, not do anything about it. And when we finally made
great waves he said, 'All right, I'll appoint an assessment
committee. All the executive'—that's the seniors—'you're the
assessment committee'. And they spent seven months and all they
did was redesign the report card. That was it. No change of policy.
And that's a big thing in the staff. The staff resent things, that are
really pupil-decisive things, where they're not allowed to make
decisions; and yet the executive whose job it is won't make
decisions on.

*Have the staff got any input into the running of the school
collectively?*

If it's a subject department decision. You talk to your subject
master, and generally they'll do it. But for the whole school
decisions, the Boss will either make the decision, or the executive,
the seniors, will make the decision. Very occasionally we'll be
consulted at a staff meeting. But the Boss will have his mind made
up. And if we agree with the Boss then he'll say, 'Well that's what
you voted on, that's what we'll do'. It looks democratic.

What is going on here is quite characteristic. The majority of
staff have little input into general policy-making (even less at
the private schools), though they are likely to have more control
over what happens at the level of their own subject department.
So far as a collective policy-making process occurs it is mainly
among the senior staff. In some schools a definite though
informal 'establishment' forms, particularly of department heads
who have been in the school a long time; Terry Petersen (chapter
2), who is part of such a group, calls himself one of the 'longest
reigning monarchs'. When the principal is in sympathy with and
operates through such a group, the rest of the staff can find
themselves excluded from the real decision-making.

What Jack Ryan paints as a pseudo-democratic stance by the
principal is one sign of a shift of management techniques in the
face of teacher professionalism and deepened divisions among
teachers. The demand for professional autonomy quickly implies
a claim for a collegial rather than a military approach to control
of the school, at least of its educational policy. At the same time

there has been increasing division among teachers about the aims and methods of teaching. Principals are more likely to find themselves in situations like Jack Ryan's principal, faced with a staff already factionalised along progressive/conservative lines, and obliged to mediate between them. Coming down heavily on one side or the other would produce real hostility in the staff— even a mild progressivism, as Jack notes, is 'not popular with a lot of people'.

The need to shift to more consensual, open-textured methods is beautifully summarised in a famous memorandum on 'Freedom and Authority in the Schools' sent to state school principals in 1970 by the Director-General of Education in South Australia:

> In exercising your authority and freedom to run your school as you think fit, of necessity you must have the backing of your staff. Without their support and participation and their adequate preparation, any departures from tradition will have little chance of success... Staff members will more readily follow a course of action if they have been taken into confidence and have shared in formulating the policy.

So important policy questions now get onto staff-meeting agendas, and principals have to explain themselves and try to win assent. Staff meetings even vote, though what follows from the vote is not always clear.

There are still many ways in which the school's administration can try to keep control of the process. The principal usually chairs the meeting and controls the agenda, and can do things like holding contentious items back until five minutes to four when everyone wants to go home. Less obviously manipulative is having new proposals screened by a meeting of senior staff before they come to general staff meetings. Only those already approved by seniors come forward, and the result is that in most cases approval is a foregone conclusion. Theo Georges is one of the younger teachers who are effectively excluded by this process:

> At this school it's fairly obvious that if you're not a senior then very little regard is paid to whatever you've got to say. Unless you're a very outspoken critic, a constant outspoken critic.
> *Are there constant outspoken critics in this school?*
> Oh, there might be half a dozen, less than that, who make changes and expect them to be brought up at meetings. But somebody will get up and immediately make them sound not as significant.

This is one reason why schools often seem blocked, unresponsive, and slow to change. The teachers who are closest to the kids, and most likely to understand what impact the school's programme is having on them, are the least able to influence school policy.

In the private schools the rise of teacher professionalism has also led to changes in management style, though one could not say that a principle of democratic control had any weight, even symbolic, in any of the private schools we studied. The shift, rather, has been towards more formal delegation, a handing-over of specific tasks and authority from the principal to other teachers, so that there is a more clear-cut division of labour in the management of the school. Less depends on personal relationships and the principal's likes and dislikes.

Teachers are a minority of the people in schools; the relations among them are always worked out against the backdrop of relations with the kids. It is interesting that Faye Taylor's account of how Greenway High operates (p. 131) gives equal weight to the involvement of the students, and immediately raises the issue of control of the curriculum. Her argument that the school's work crucially depends on the 'co-operation' of the students is plainly true. An important part of the political order of a school, therefore, has to do with how this co-operation is gained, and how students who refuse to give it are handled.

This is the school-wide aspect of the discipline questions discussed at a person-to-person level in chapter 8; but it involves more than just the imposition of a disciplinary regime. How the school's disciplinary regime works depends to a significant degree on an interplay between the school's hegemonic curriculum and its catchment.

Faye Taylor notes how students play games to get out of work, but 'they expect results so they're prepared to do some'. In a streamed high school where the academic curriculum is hegemonic, the kids who have best reason to 'expect results' are those in the top streams. These are the kids for whom the academic curriculum is working well and who are being favoured by the school's selection mechanisms. Their purposes are likely to coincide with the teachers', and the result is likely to be a well-established hegemony of the staff in upper-stream classes. This can happen whether the teacher's technique is pupil-centred or teacher-centred.

Whether that hegemony is local, confined to the top streams, or becomes the basis of the political order of the whole school, is variable. It depends, in part, on changes in the school's intake. One of the schools we studied was right on the urban fringe; it had formerly had a more rural catchment, and teachers noted how the problems of control had grown as its intake became more purely urban. Another had formerly been a regional selective school, with a strongly academic programme and a high degree of compliance from the kids. Conversion to a local comprehensive school had rapidly eroded the hegemony of the school's programme and was one of the forces producing what the teachers felt as a crisis of discipline in the school.

The political problems that arise from such processes are well shown by the vicissitudes of student representation. In the wake of the student movement a decade or so ago, there has been a trend towards replacing prefect systems with representative councils of some kind. Margaret Atwill tells the story of the year her school went radical and introduced a Students' Representative Council (SRC), with elected delegates from all forms. Margaret, from the perspective of a deputy, declares that it 'was fairly unsuccessful', because the students 'chose very poorly'. What happened was that, perhaps seeing that the SRC had no power, they elected some stirrers. In Margaret's account a couple of them came to dominate the SRC and put other people off coming to the meetings, especially the younger kids. At the end of the year the principal abolished the SRC and went back to having prefects. These too are elected, though from the senior school only, and see their main role as organising dances. Margaret is much happier with the choices the kids are making now.

In the private schools a large measure of compliance by the kids is more or less guaranteed, for reasons already explored. This can break down in exceptional circumstances. The Vietnam war created such a crisis in some of the boys' private schools, with open resistance to the previously sacred cadet corps. Another circumstance that led to a collapse of good order and decorum was the last years of a head who was losing grip and interest. But in general the problem is not lack of order. It may even be the reverse. Heavy-handed and effective discipline can create problems of motivation, of getting the students to show initiative, to strike out on their own. Glen Moncrieff is one private school teacher who feels quite strongly that his school is too inbred and overprotective for the kids' own good. They do not get a breadth of perspective on the world, and they do not necessarily get much intellectual stimulation either:

> I think really, here, there's far too much straight teaching. Without trying to stimulate. And surely that's what teaching is all about.

Not all his colleagues agree. But enough do to suggest that there is indeed a negative side to 'good order' in schools. As Sheila Goffman (chapter 1) discovered that learning does not necessarily happen in a quiet classroom where the kids jump when the teacher says 'Jump', so the best education need not be happening in the most orderly schools.

I have described the political order of a school as a 'state of play'; schools change, however much they seem not to. Sometimes they change simply because they are under pressure and something gives, like the effects of changed catchments already mentioned. Sometimes the change is catastrophic; Joe Welton recalls events at a tough high school early in his teaching career (in the 1950s):

> We had a weak headmaster and we had a collapse of discipline.
> Smashed toilets. Assaulted people. The staff went down. I
> remember one class there, of thirty-three I had nineteen on bond.
> And that was very rugged.

In such circumstances the Department may send in an equally tough principal. Ralph Duffy recalls such an episode from earlier in the history of Greenway High. A new head was brought in to 'tidy it up'. Staff and students respected him. If a teacher was coping with the situation he or she would be left alone, and if not, the Boss would step in. He did the job, tightened up the school.

This is an equivalent, in the public school system, of something that is more conspicuous in the private schools, the way a school can change by deliberate *renovation* from the top. In four of the private schools we studied this had happened in the recent past, and we heard of other cases as teachers were talking of their experiences with other schools. There is a kind of formula which private school people use to describe the process. The school becomes slack, loses ground in the market, teacher and student morale falls, parents contemplate withdrawing their children; the school is 'in a mess', as one reforming headmistress put it. The school council brings in a new principal, who recruits new staff, gets rid of some of the old staff—the 'dead wood' as one supporter of a reforming headmaster put it—and starts cracking down on the kids, having blitzes on school rules, and beefing up the academic programme. If all goes well, the school's fortunes revive and the new head's reputation is established.

This process can be turned to very different ends. A school can be renovated to modernise it, to emphasise the profession-alism of the teachers and the academic success of the kids. Where this happens in a girls' school it can be the vehicle of quite radical views on equality for women. On the other hand a private school, most of which are officially church foundations, can be renovated to emphasise conventional religion, social conformity, family life and 'moral standards'. And the process often runs into trouble. The new head may have to attack vested interests in the school, including strongly entrenched senior staff, and can easily antagonise some groups of parents. Tightening discipline is likely to antagonise the kids. Teachers who are not part of the reforming group may feel very insecure, as candidates for 'dead wood' status. One teacher in such a position whom we spoke to remarked on the 'raw deals' handed out to staff recently got rid of. The bloodletting may result in lawsuits; in counter-attacks on the new principal, which can be quite vicious; or in a reform which damages the school because too many of the good teachers leave.

So there are forces for conservation even in the context of conscious change. Where a school seems not to change at all, it is because its internal arrangements, for the time being, give the upper hand to these forces. To return to Theo Georges (p. 00):

> The seniors—I shouldn't generalise here, but I think they're more rigid, more conservative. And when you say, 'Look, let's do this because of that', they'll say, 'Look we've tried it. This is what the book says'. They've got all the answers. 'I'm the senior, I know it', this sort of business. Whereas you say, 'Well, look, you know, I don't care whether that's right or not, this is what I want to do'. Usually you find that there's the pressure. Not that that bothers me, because when I'm in the classroom I'm the guy that runs the class whether they like it or not. This is what I'm getting paid for. So, sometimes there is this pressure, which is fair enough, to give consistency to the school.

Theo accepts a need 'to give consistency to the school', to coordinate teachers' practices, in relation to discipline as well as the curriculum. No reasonable teacher would deny that. What he and others like him are upset about is the *way* the coordination is done. The effect of the practices of Theo's school is to create a heavy atmosphere of caution, as much a sense of fatigue as of conscious conservatism.

Underpinning this is a system of arrangements that concentrates power in the hands of people who are older, further up the bureaucratic hierarchy, more skilled in the craft aspects of teaching, almost all Anglo, and almost all men. There is nothing unusual about Australian schools in this; Town, for instance, outlines an eerily similar pattern in Scottish schools as the basis of their complacency and resistance to reform.[6] A number of social hierarchies overlap within a school, and it is difficult to tell where one ends and the next begins. Over the course of a teaching lifetime these relationships get embedded in one's identity, like the strategies for control of kids. So the holders of authority have the best of all motives to resist challenges to it: they are defending themselves. No wonder there is the 'pressure' Theo feels; no wonder his school has had serious trouble renovating itself to meet a changed set of circumstances. Public schools can be renovated, but their organisation makes it very difficult to do from below.

The gender regime

An aspect of schools that has only intermittently come into focus in the past is the way they institutionalise gender relations, handle questions of sexuality and sexual identity, encourage particular forms of femininity and masculinity and discourage others. Such issues have not been wholly ignored, but they have typically been discussed under very restrictive headings: notably coeducation *vs* single-sex schooling, and parental *vs* teacher control of 'sex education'. Recent research on gender relations makes it possible to see these as parts of a much larger set of questions.[7]

The pattern of gender relations institutionalised in a school I will call its 'gender regime'. The way it embodies patterns of authority is an important part of the political order of the school. The association that our society makes between authority and masculinity, more specifically adult heterosexual masculinity, is a significant underpinning of the power structure of a school system where most administrators, principals and subject heads are men. It can create difficulty when women are exercising authority, even so well-institutionalised a form of authority as being headmistress of a girls' school. A cool observer on the staff of one noted how its headmistress readily took to task the women on her staff, but did not do that with the men.

Gender relations inside a school are of course interwoven with those outside. The sexual division of labour is one of the major features of a school's gender regime; and it is clear that the sexual division of labour described in chapter 6 conforms with larger social patterns. Women as secretaries and in other support functions, men predominating among administrators; women teaching home science and predominating in the 'soft' subjects, the humanities, while men teach carpentry and metalwork, and predominate in the 'hard' sciences, maths and technology—this is all rather familiar. So are the conventions underlying the ways schools mark out gender divisions for their pupils: uniforms (skirts and blouses *vs* slacks and shirts), sports (netball *vs* football), forms of address ('Yes, Miss'), curriculum tracks and electives (typing *vs* technical drawing), and so on. At Greenway High for many years there was an invisible line down the middle of the playground: girls were supposed to stay on one side, boys on the other. 'It worked', says Doris Willoughby laconically.

But the line is now gone, and Doris for one is not sorry. While the school is influenced by larger social patterns, it also has some room to decide what it does with them. Indeed it is arguable that that 'invisible line' was not so much a reflection of the wider social pattern as a marked exaggeration of it. Women and men are not segregated completely in everyday life. And in recent years there has been a strong shift in the other direction. While some schools still insist on skirts for the girls, others now allow slacks or even jeans. What used to be a totally sex-segregated activity, 'sport', is now in many schools a largely integrated (and much more varied) physical education programme.

Practice within a school is not likely to be wholly consistent. A school attempting to encourage girls into maths and sciences may still have mostly men teaching these subjects. Conflict may be open when feminist teachers run up against unsupportive or actively hostile men in positions of authority in the school. We saw this several times. Arlette Anderson, for instance, came into conflict with her principal in her first year out; she commented wryly that she saw him as a male chauvinist and he saw her as a female chauvinist.

Some schools can live with a good deal of incoherence or even conflict on gender issues. In others a more determined effort is made to produce a consistent gender regime. Some examples of this have been mentioned already, for instance Julius Abernethy's concern to keep out teachers who are openly homosexual or promiscuous (p. 130). Julius describes his school's sex education programme as propaganda for the family:

> It's got a Christian emphasis on the fact that the family is a
> God-given thing, therefore it is to be prized, and therefore the way
> we use what is basically a family thing [sex] should be in that
> context.

This is, indeed, part of a more general attempt at control and direction of the students' social relations and sexuality. This kind of effort appears much more characteristic of the private than of the public schools.

Most of the private schools are segregated. This used to be a point where market demand and the schools' own ideology coincided. Now there is rather more division on both fronts. Segregated girls' private schools are still defended, by some of the teachers we spoke to, on the grounds that the girls achieve better without distraction from boys. Others, however, are sceptical of this argument and regard segregated schools as inhibiting the girls' social development. Angela Ruskin is one who made this criticism practical. She took her daughters out of the segregated private school where she worked and put them in a state school so they would develop 'normal relationships' with boys.

In a number of ways, issues of sexuality and gender seem to have become increasing sources of difficulty and turbulence for the schools. In this, of course, schools are not alone. The era of women's liberation and gay liberation, effective contraception and markedly greater sexual freedoms, has seen the gender regimes of many institutions under pressure. The high school is inevitably a focus of this pressure, as an institution dealing with large concentrations of adolescents. It has so far conceded freer expression of sexual interest among the kids, and a considerable weakening of social segregation. It is involved in larger changes in the sexual division of labour, mainly by having encouraged increasing numbers of girls to stay to matriculation and hence have the change of entering the professional end of the labour market. It has not changed much in its own sexual division of labour or in its endorsement of the ideology of gender division. These are perhaps the next areas for change.

The school's milieu

Schools are transparent places. Anyone can walk in and see what is going on. Teachers may spend much of their time in class-rooms isolated from their fellow-workers, but in each of these rooms are twenty or thirty pairs of eyes and ears, and twenty or thirty tongues to talk about it afterwards. Twice a day all adjourn to playground or staffroom and discuss how things are going. Information and rumour pass around a school easily; and most kids talk to their families about what they do and hear in school.

Teachers are, understandably, sensitive to surveillance from parents. Mary Coleman puts it pungently:

> Let's face it, most teachers are only too well aware that if they say anything about politics or religion they're likely to have an irate parent breathing down their neck! And that's happened a few times, the next day complaining. So I think most teachers are aware that they've got to not take sides. Kids will say to me 'What party do you vote for?' and I say 'It's none of your business'. I'm not going to put my neck on a chopping block and get into political arguments over something like that.

So it is not easy to do the kind of teaching about the real political world that Mary wants to do (see pp. 96–7). Not many parents at a working-class school like this actually feel confident enough to steam up to the school and bang on the table. But even 'a few times' is embarrassing for the school administration, and upsetting for the teacher, not to mention the teacher's career. The prudent strategy, as Mary has learnt, is to keep mum.

Pressure from the parents is not confined to controversial topics. I have quoted Margaret Blackall's view (pp. 16–7) that the parents she deals with at Greenway High do not value intellect and knowledge for its own sake, but want their kids to be trained for jobs. She is right on the second point. Our interviews were done at a time of rising youth unemployment, and the parents' anxieties on this score were perfectly realistic. (Where they went wrong was in *over*-estimating what the schools could do for their kids at a time of labour market collapse.) The main effect of this pressure, in the view of teachers like Terry Petersen (chapter 2), has been to reinforce the school's attachment to exams and academic competition, and therefore to reinforce the traditional hierarchy of subjects. In short it has bolstered the hegemony of the competitive academic curriculum at a time when that curriculum was more patently failing the majority of kids than ever before.

Teachers' responses to pressure from parents varies between three main positions. Andrew Sutting, the computer buff, is firmly at one end: he sees much of the school's attempt to involve parents as quite tokenistic, a public-relations exercise on the part of the principal. He thinks teachers have more import-ant things to do with their time, and would like parents to keep their distance. James Christianson, principal of one of the pri-vate schools, makes sure that they do. He has a well–developed technique for fending off stroppy parents, pointing out that when their child started they were told how the school runs, and asking if they were deceived? They have to answer 'no'. He then points out to them that if they take a matter to their lawyer, they place it in the lawyer's hands and don't try to tell him what is the law; and it is the same with schools...

Tom Jones, an old hand in the state schools, illustrates a second position. Most teachers have little or no contact with parents, he notes, and prefer it that way for good practical reasons:

> I'd have to take more time to explain to parents, and as parents
> will be like kids here I'd be continually explaining. They get things
> mixed up, wouldn't understand, and I wouldn't be able to
> concentrate. As well I'd have to take time from somewhere to
> make time. It'd be from the kids. Then you'd have a double set of
> problems.

Yet Tom thinks that parents should have easier access than they do now. He dislikes the present system where all parents' enquiries are channelled through the principal, arguing that they should be able to go 'direct to the teachers'.

Joe Milwell illustrates a third position. While critical of parents for their lack of active involvement—

> It's only when you've reached the last stage fight with the child
> and you're thinking of suspending them or expelling them or
> something, that you get those parents out of their holes and down
> to the school. It's a rather sad fact really. Probably is lack of
> parental concern.

—he does not fall back on the belief that teachers should therefore run the schools on the strength of their professional knowledge. He is committed to genuine power-sharing:

> I see a school's role more as a community school than part of a
> bureaucratic system.

He is critical of teachers and bureaucrats too when they get in
the way of this. What is needed, in Joe's view, are strong school
councils that accept responsibility not only for finance but also
for curriculum. They would be the focus of a cohesive school
community, one which encouraged lots of direct contact between
teachers and parents. They would also be in a position to make
realistic curriculum decisions in relation to the kids' need to get
jobs.

Joe's position is the least common of the three, but it is
important as it is based on the possibility of the state school
becoming organic to the working-class community. At the
moment, few are. The main external force acting on the state
school as a workplace is not the local community but the larger
education system, and particularly the Department.

The state Departments of Education bulk so large in the
politics of Australian education, and have been discussed so
often, that it is difficult to say anything fresh about them.
Perhaps the main thing to be said here is how little the Department came up in our material. It is there as background; but for
most of the public school teachers most of the time it is background taken for granted. There has been a historical shift away
from heavy-handed bureaucracy. Grace remarks on a parallel
movement in the control of urban education in England, away
from 'visible and centralized control' towards 'invisible and
diffused control'.[9]

Changes of policy did stir comment. At about the time we
were interviewing, the Department in South Australia had
adopted a policy of support for unstreamed classes; several of
the South Australian teachers we talked to grumbled about the
trouble this was causing. But as schools had ways of sidestepping

this policy, the trouble was not very great.

In fact the most strident complaints about the Department all came from *private* school teachers, who did not themselves have to deal with it. Some were from teachers who had previously been in the public system, and who cited bureaucratic rigidity, forced transfers, and appointments in distant schools among their reasons for getting out. But the same complaints about the Department were also made by teachers who had not been in the public system at all. Without denying that these episodes are true, or pretending that big bureaucracies are models of human kindness, it is also true that these things are said in a political context of antagonism to public schooling.

Since the expansion of public secondary schooling broke the private schools' pre-war near-monopoly of matriculation, the private schools' position in the market and as claimants for state aid has increasingly come to depend on their ability to present themselves as a desirable *alternative*. That inevitably means running down the competition. Private school teachers often talk of the state schools in somewhat horrified tones; and vilification of the bureaucracy that controls them is a natural part of the picture. It fits happily with the larger theme of conservative ideology that vilifies 'bureaucratic' control of the economy and praises 'free enterprise' for its dynamism, diversity, and encouragement of free choice.

Accordingly the notion of 'parental choice' has become an important theme in conservative rhetoric about education. In *Making the Difference* we stressed the significance of the market for the elite private schools as an economic mechanism which linked them to a ruling-class clientele while giving them some room to manoeuvre in overcoming narrowly-defined class interests. That argument needs to be qualified by the importance of state aid; it was access to the state that bailed out private schooling from its economic crisis in the 1960s. Yet this in turn points to the importance of the ideological devices providing legitimacy for private schooling; and it is clear that the market is now central as an ideological mechanism.

Julius Abernethy clearly illustrates how, when talking about whether his school should introduce a Transition Education course for kids who obviously will not matriculate.

Does that mean you suggest that perhaps there's bias here to academic, or university entrance?

No—ah—yes. I think that—not in the junior years—I'm not sure what our role should be. I'm still feeling my way in this one, with the senior years, whether we should be offering a broader spectrum of subjects or whether we should just say look, you know, this school doesn't cater for that. Let's take a case of Wellington College who say very definitely we do not cater for the non-academic student in the senior years and that's it; so that unless he's got much chance of gaining entrance to university, he won't get in, that's what happens there. No, I'm not sure exactly what our role is here. I think the law of supply and demand is possibly the only guidance we can get, because obviously if we're going to pay our way, we have to have x number of students. Now what do parents want for them? We have to try and supply it I suppose.

The market is connected with the school's programme and with school authority, and the armature connecting them is 'parental choice'. No large educational purposes of enlightenment, cultural renewal, or the like here; the market makes the hard curriculum decisions for you.

This is not a realistic description of a world where curricula are still partly determined centrally (for instance via matriculation syllabuses) and materials like textbooks are often standardised across schools. Nor would many teachers go so far in thinking that the market *should* settle things. Glen Moncrieff, who is an equally firm supporter of private schooling, waxes sardonic about the market and parents' attempts to maximise their kids' advantages:

They've got to justify spending a hell of a lot of money when they don't have to spend it otherwise [i.e. in the state system]. You know, the great god Dollar comes into things a *lot* in private school education.

It is still true that the private school's relation to the market strongly affects the terms in which educational issues are posed. The question of non-academic curricula for Year 11 and 12 (p. 96) is an important current example.

The greatly increased prominence of the notion of parental choice in the legitimation of private schooling illustrates another general point. Schools' relationships with their environment keep changing, because the environment keeps changing. For three decades the schools were under pressure because the demand for secondary education kept rising; in the late 1970s it levelled off. The famous Departmental regimentation itself is increasingly a thing of the past. New management techniques have affected education departments too; and regionalisation, school-based curricula, school-controlled assessment, community control and worker control are all on the public education scene. The ethnic composition of the working class has changed radically over a generation. The established order of gender relations has cracked here and there. Ruling-class parents have become more demanding as the competition for university places has tightened. Kids are more sceptical of authority, harder to control.

It is easy enough for teachers to feel under siege from social change; to feel, as Angus Barr says about contact with parents (p. 143), that 'no news is good news'. It is important, then, to find ways of thinking about schools, and organising teachers' work, that overcome the tendency to erect barriers around the school and cultivate a teachers' quiet place behind them. Joe Milwell's argument about parent involvement (p. 143) has a larger significance here. It is not a matter of blocking out uncomfortable social pressures and social changes. It is rather a question of coming to terms with them, realistically, and turning the encounter to good educational purpose.

Summary, chapter 9

There is a formal structure of supervision within schools. How closely it impinges on teachers' work varies a good deal, and surveillance is more insistent in the private schools. It may be seen as part of the *political order* of the school as an institution. A common pattern of school politics is for effective decision-making to rest in the hands of a group of senior staff with fairly nominal involvement of the rest, though there has been a historical trend towards more participatory management. The hierarchies of power tend to reinforce educational conservatism. Student compliance is usual in upper streams, very much at issue in lower streams, and at times can break down generally. There is a process of reestablishing order by top-down renovation, particularly noticeable in private schools. A key aspect of a school's political order is its *gender regime*, involving the sexual division of labour, the ordering of masculinity and femininity, etc. This has become a significant point of tension, partly because of interaction with social forces outside the school. Teachers respond to pressure from parents in a range of ways, mostly somewhat defensive, though there are some who support active parent involvement. Outside pressure also comes through the Department and through the market. The latter has become an increasingly important ideological mechanism in ruling-class education. Schools' relationships to their environment change historically, and can become the object of conscious practice.

Part Three
Teachers' Worlds

10

Being a teacher

The sense of self

The argument has laid a good deal of emphasis on the emotional
dimension of teachers' work. This is something that has consequences for their conceptions of themselves and for the way
they function as people.

With teachers well on in a career this is likely to appear as a
blurring, sometimes a rather eerie identity, of the job and the
person. This is not necessarily a total absorption of the person
into the rôle, as in *Goodbye, Mr Chips*. The rôle is not as settled
as that. Rather, the way one responds to the emotional demands
of teaching becomes decisive for one's whole emotional
economy.

Angus Barr (chapter 3), the oldest of the teachers discussed in
part I, shows one form of this. Margaret Atwill, deputy at
Greenway High, shows another. Her path in life has been
centred on constructing a career in teaching; and a teaching style
and educational outlook based on the principle of hastening
slowly, of cautious realism, comes through as a philosophy of
life informing her whole outlook on the world. Mary Coleman is
a young teacher who can see this kind of thing happening to her
elders and is not too happy about it:

> This is my fourth year out, and finally I think I'm starting to
> become a reasonable teacher. It's taken me three years to get to
> this stage, so there's got to be lots of room for improvement yet!
> But I honestly don't know; I still—I hate the idea of becoming one
> of these elderly lady teachers in twenty years' time, it's a fairly
> horrifying prospect. But I don't know. I suppose I could go into
> something else.

But there is nothing else in prospect.

Another person who has a strong sense of the relationship between teaching and personal style is the analytic Faye Taylor. She puts it like this:

> I think it is much easier to teach for a person who likes ordering people around. Somebody who naturally likes to boss the show.
> Then it is fairly easy to order children and keep them doing exactly what you want. But I'm never quite sure what I want.

What does it do to Faye, to have to spend most of her working life 'ordering people around' when she does not feel comfortable doing that? What does it do to Margaret Blackall (chapter 1), to have to administer a system of grading and streaming which causes so much distress to the young? Teachers' capacity to care is important. And teaching, as well as having joys, also means failing kids, streaming them down, creating a good deal of boredom and frustration, and inflicting occasional punishments. In short, it involves inflicting a good deal of pain. This must have its effects on teachers in the long run.

One understandable response is to blunt one's capacity to care. Settled teachers often speak of their jobs, their schools, and their pupils in a sceptical, even cynical, way that can be quite startling when encountered for the first time. Teachers who have risen in their careers, especially men, often develop a style of bluff, humorous ruthlessness that puts the problems of teaching in the same pocket as the problems of management. Other teachers carve out a niche for themselves and retreat into it: the art room, the computing programme, or whatever. And many others back off from emotional involvement in their work, drawing lines around what they will and will not do, parcelling themselves up:

> My three priorities have always been health first, family second, and school third. And when you've got them out of gear you've got problems.

On the other hand there are teachers who refuse to be defensive, who open themselves to the ebb and flow and respond with the full range of their personal resources. Sheila Goffman (chapter 1), Rosa Marshall (chapter 4), Joe Milwell (p. 123) have very different personal styles and educational outlooks, but all are engaged in this kind of way. The willingness to be engaged carries a clear risk of being absorbed, or at least of being burnt out. The protection which Rosa and Joe both have, and which

Sheila is perhaps beginning to develop, is a kind of realism which enables them to take a critical view of their situations without collapsing into cynicism. That kind of realism is a most valuable property. It would be nice if there were some way of teaching it in the DipEd.

Femininity and masculinity

I argued in chapter 1 that Sheila Goffman's way of being a teacher, her personal version of progressivism, expresses something about her identity as a woman. As the structure of gender relations is one of the major social forces shaping education, so patterns of femininity and masculinity are an important part of the personal context of teaching.

Neither femininity nor masculinity is a simple or uniform thing. There are various ways of inhabiting the social identity of a woman or of a man, and none of them is completely free of tensions and contradictions. Being a teacher involves a complex interplay of these aspects of personality with the structure of the job.

Margaret Blackall, for instance (chapter 1), shows a well-developed capacity to empathise, to 'care about kids' in a direct as well as an abstract way. This aspect of her work calls into play the capacities and sympathies that our society considers to be feminine and summarises in the notion of 'mothering'. At the same time she has to establish her authority over them, achieve order in the classroom, enforce school rules, impose discipline.

There is a tension here which is more than an incompatibility between two practices. It is a tension about gender itself. Authority, in our society, is felt to be masculine; to assert it is to undermine one's femininity, in other people's eyes and often in one's own. The strength of this patriarchal convention is shown by the fact that while professions such as medicine have now been opened on a fair scale to women, business management—which involves above all the assertion of authority against resistance—has not. The contradiction it creates in teaching is registered in the creation of derogatory comic stereotypes of women teachers: the rigid spinster school-marm, the tweedy hockey-mistress, and so on.

A woman teacher discovers fairly early whether she can enforce classroom discipline or not; as her teaching experience grows, another classic dilemma emerges. In a society where very little provision for long-term childcare is made except the unpaid labour of mothers, a conflict about motherhood is set up for women in a career. It is only 50 years since an Act of Parliament dismissed married women *en bloc* from the NSW teaching service, to protect jobs for men during the Depression.[10] Promotion in the state systems has long depended on availability for country service, almost an impossibility for married women as few husbands will give up their jobs to follow a wife's career. Someone like Margaret Atwill, entering teaching in the 1940s, effectively had to choose between marriage and career. She was unusual in approaching the job in a career-minded way from the start, and the result was that she never married, in a generation when almost all Australian women did.

Whether to have children is a lively issue for younger women teachers. Lorraine Smart, who has been a teacher for two years, puts it clearly:

We were just talking about that in the staff-room, funnily enough; and I think the general consensus of opinion amongst we female teachers was that we will probably have reached the menopause by the time we were to have children! It's a very big problem for a woman who wants a career plus children as well—unless you want other people to raise your children.
You want a career?
Yes.
What does a career mean to you?
It means the opportunity to do things that I want to do, the ability to rise to a challenge outside the home. I'm not saying that motherhood isn't necessarily creative. I can see motherhood as a very pleasant and perhaps creative time—I'm not really sure about that—later on, when I want to settle down. I'm not settled yet. I don't want to enclose myself within four walls of a house. And I feel that I've got something useful to do here. And I like the independence of earning my own money, and at the same time I feel that I can meet my husband as an equal, and I can enjoy our marriage as something separate from all this. I think it enriches our marriage, because we've both got different worlds to talk about, and we are both a shelter and a comfort to each other, I think. Whereas I don't think I would be as nice if I had to stay at home. And I don't think I would be as stimulated as I am here. I don't think I would be an interesting person at all.

Mary Coleman, who could have been part of that staffroom conversation, considers it would be a waste of good training to spend her time 'changing nappies and washing dishes'; an attitude shared by many men.

Quite a number of the women teachers we spoke to had been engaged in rethinking their position as women and the accepted conventions of gender. They range from those who make a full-blooded critique of marriage, like Alison Chant and Rosa Marshall, through those who are trying to thrash out some model of egalitarian marriage, like Lorraine Smart, to those who are simply enjoying small departures, like Bettina Alt who tells with pride of her adult son's skill at sewing.

If teaching has aspects that are not easily reconciled with traditional femininity, it is not unambiguously masculine either. As jobs go, this is generally regarded as a soft one. The element of emotional engagement, and indeed emotional manipulation, that is inevitable in teaching, is defined as feminine in our culture. Caring for children is, other things being equal, regarded as women's work. The stress particular schools lay on arts and music, pastoral care or religion is at odds with some versions of traditional masculinity. Alan Watson, who believes that 'in First Form you terrify them' (p. 104) and spends his own leisure in the Army reserve, is irritated by that aspect of his school. He thinks its 'spoon-fed' kids will have a terrible shock when they hit the business world after all this mollycoddling.

As Alan's tough treatment of his own classes suggests, one way of handling this is to emphasise aspects of teaching that are more compatible with conventional masculinity. Discipline, even if it is over children, is the assertion of authority. The element of violence in the traditional disciplinary regime is emphatically masculine: it is mainly boys who are hit with the cane, and mainly men who hit them. Further up the career ladder, authority is exercised over adults as a department head, deputy, or principal. This is not only compatible with conventional masculinity, it amplifies and confirms it. Teachers like Angus Barr (chapter 3) and James Christianson (p. 142) have achieved a marriage of masculinity and authoritativeness which makes personal style and exercise of power seem natural aspects of each other.

In our interviews there seemed to be more deliberate concern with masculinity and its problems in the private schools; but the inflection of teaching to emphasise its masculine side is certainly found in state schools too. Andrew Sutting has quite successfully done this. Upwardly mobile from a working-class family, he went into maths and science, did a stint in the army, went through a trial by fire in a really tough technical school, and has got as close as you can to high technology in teaching by becoming a computer specialist (p. 85). It is not so surprising to find him a supporter of corporal punishment (p. 110), and in personal style unemotional and self-controlled. While being aware of the issues raised by feminists, and no unthinking reactionary, Andrew responds to a question on childcare and shared parenting with a quite unselfconscious 'I'd be bored'.

But this kind of solution is criticised by other men. Jeremy Hansen is one. He is sharply critical of his school's stress on football, and the pressure put on boys of unsuitable physique to play it because 'it's the manly thing to do'. This is not just a verbal critique, either, as Jeremy now refuses to act as a football coach, a usual requirement at his school.

A number of the men we interviewed were at least ambivalent about the exercise of masculine authority in the school setting. Glen Moncrieff, for instance, is involved in scouts, school cadets, and so on; but insists that scouts is pointless without social mixing and that he is in the cadets to teach the kids bushcraft and self-reliance. Clive Brimcombe, a progressive teacher in an academically-oriented girls' school, has been getting into real difficulty with his classes by deliberately trying to abandon masculine authority. He makes himself vulnerable by laying his own feelings on the line, and attempts to involve his pupils in a non-directive teaching style. Len Johnson, who thinks the kids regard him as a 'soft touch' but does not have Clive's kind of trouble on his hands, is perhaps managing the retreat better.

There is little evidence here of a reconstruction of masculinity on the scale of the reconstruction of femininity going on among women teachers influenced by feminism. There are certainly men, such as Andy Gallea, who take a more relaxed attitude to their masculine dignity. On one occasion Andy donned ballet tights and danced a number from *Swan Lake* at the school concert, to the delirious pleasure of the kids. No doubt he is helped by being a physical education teacher, with an unchallengeable claim to masculinity of the more physical kind. The conscious shedding of authority, of Clive Brimcombe's kind, remains rare and fraught with difficulty.

It still seems reasonable to suggest that hegemonic masculinity has come under increasing strain in the last decade,[11] and that teachers are involved in this. The emotional contradictions of teaching have become more difficult for men to resolve, or at least cannot be resolved in ways that once seemed natural and unchallengeable. The maintenance of highly patriarchal gender regimes and the production of masculinity in the schools puts a strain on the teachers as well as the boys, that is perhaps increasing.

John Welton, a conservative teacher in a conservative boys' private school, seems a model of patriarchal attitudes, strong on discipline and regimentation, a firm supporter of the cadets. But when asked what he would do if he were principal, after stressing academic work, he goes on:

> The second thing would be to have a very strong cultural school. I would like to think that any school that I ran had a piano going constantly and that you should be able to hear it. Theatre, choral, verse speaking, the lot. Because I think we are in an age now which is pretty violent, and I think the schools have a part to play here, by showing by sensitive and civilised behaviour that this sort of thing is abhorrent.

And even more striking, he would love to teach in a coeducational school.

> Everyone I've talked to says that it's excellent. I've taught too long in boys' schools. I think girls are more sensible than boys. I think the male in our era is declining, females are coming into their own. I'm not a women's liberationist but I'd like to teach girls just to see what it's like. And I think, when I see them in buses and so on, and I see my own daughters, and I think 'how much more sensible'.

Teaching as a path in life

Both the technical and the emotional strands of teaching are woven in with the pattern of a career.

The teachers we interviewed came into teaching mainly along three paths. Some became teachers because they were pushed, or pulled, by their families. Ralph Duffy grew up in a rural working-class family who could afford to send just one child on to further education. He was the one his mother chose. With others, the family was important because it provided models. Faye Taylor's mother was a teacher, her father was a headmaster. At first Faye wanted to be anything but a teacher, but eventually she succumbed.

Margaret Atwill's parents were against her becoming a teacher. She came into it because she was promoted by an academic high school. She was one of a number of teachers who were, in effect, recruited by their own teachers. Angela Ruskin was encouraged by two stimulating art teachers, at a time when there was lots of 'pressure' from the Education Department in her state to get more teachers. Some of the private school teachers were recruited by their former principals to teach in their former schools.

A third group of teachers chose teaching after some experience in other jobs. Joe Milwell, after a crisis in his family life, was looking for alternatives; some friends suggested he would be a natural as a teacher, he was surprised but agreed, and retrained. James Fenimore, watching his boss drive himself into a heart attack, decided he wanted something slower paced, so threw up his career in manufacturing and went teaching.

There are several implications of these entry routes. First, the recruitment of teachers by other teachers, especially through classroom success or attendance at a selective state school, is one of the practices underpinning teachers' attachment to the competitive academic curriculum. This is more than the obvious fact that teachers are people who were good at academic work. For a significant number of them, academic competition was the means of shaping their interest in the job itself.

Second, the traditional social function of teaching as a means of upward mobility from the working class still operates. Our teachers include the son of rural labourers, the daughter of a coal miner, the daughter of a cook, the son of a machinist. It is not a question of a bloc of middle-class teachers confronting working-class kids. As Sheila Goffman insists (chapter 1) 'the difference is not that we don't come from a working-class background, because some of us do'.

Those who move up in the world through formal education often go through the tensions and live out the malaise that Sennett and Cobb have taught us to see as 'the hidden injuries of class'. Margaret Blackall, as described in chapter 1, was strongly supported through school by her poorly-educated parents. But now she has made it,

> There is a gap there, because they see me as something better than they. But it's a matter of living on different levels, so when I'm there I'm on a different level. As my husband said, he wouldn't waste speeches on them. I sound different. I'm not conscious of the change, it's just there. My mother, her complaint used to be that 'Oh, you are not like me'. So it's a matter of educating her into the fact that I'm not supposed to be, but that is very hard.

Other teachers talk of similar experiences. In some cases the uprooting is an ethnic process on top of the class process. Joe Guaraldi could not speak English when he arrived in Australia as a child; now he lives largely outside the Italian community, has rejected his Catholic schooling, married an Anglo wife. Theo Georges was pushed on and out by his father, an immigrant worker in a motor plant who told him he would 'end up there working next to me' if he did not study hard.

The numbers are not large enough for statistical comparisons, but our material strongly suggests that the elite private schools recruit teachers from distinctly more affluent band of the social spectrum than the state system does. Indeed for some, being a teacher involves a kind of *downward* mobility, at least a distinct retreat from the levels of power and wealth they could have aspired to as the children of businessmen or professionals. A good many, that is to say, come from backgrounds very like those of their clients, which no doubt reinforces their sense of identity of interest. It can also lead to a discomfort among those who, like Angela Ruskin as the daughter of a country carpenter, come from a very different background.

The third point is that teachers' entry routes depend on historical circumstances. During the big expansion of secondary schooling in the 1950s and 1960s, as Len Johnson puts it,

> They just grabbed teachers from anywhere and stuck them in front of classes.

Faye Taylor came in at the same time as Len. She approached the Department for a job and was sent to a school. She observed for one day, taught two lessons on the second and third; on day four they told her the syllabus, and the following Monday they took me into the classroom, said 'This is your new teacher', and closed the door. I did not have any idea of programming, depth, timing. I didn't know what time the lessons started or ended. I didn't know any of the Departmental system; and I had not been in a classroom for eight years.

That kind of thing does not happen in the state schools any more. In fact trained teachers are now likely to face a stint of unemployment before they get a job in the schools. Recruitment of untrained teachers still occurs in the private schools, though it is probably less than it was.

Teachers differ about how valuable formal teacher training is. There is a quite widespread opinion that it is no use at all, that the DipEd is a wasted year. Especially it is no practical use: it does not prepare one for the discipline problem, and the methods courses are out of touch with classroom reality. Just one sample, from Roy Clive:

I'd say that a lot of DipEd work is pretty irrelevant anyway as far as being a teacher is concerned.
What kind of material?
Oh, well, stuff on curriculum, design of curriculum and so on. Which I think doesn't really have that much to do with the day-to-day business of teaching. Even the methods course I'm doing on science method doesn't have much to do with day-to-day teaching. It appears to me to be taught by people who haven't ever taught people in schools, not so much universities, before in their lives. Their ideas I've tried which have been total disasters...it appears to me to be a sort of idea that someone's dreamed up and hasn't really used.

Not all agree. Rosa Marshall used to share his opinion of the theory in her Diploma course. But after five years out it resurfaced, and has become more relevant as she has had to re-evaluate her methods. Joe Guaraldi cites his Diploma course as a source of his understanding of curriculum politics, and of ideas for the more pupil-centred practices of his biology class-room (p. 78).

Clearly the DipEd is not a convincing enough professional preparation to settle much about teachers' methods or outlooks. Most of the learning is still done on the job; and the First Year Out, rather than the formal training, is what teachers tend to think of as their real induction. Yet lacking the DipEd can still seem a weakness; Faye Taylor, after fifteen years, still feels her position as an untrained teacher. And further training is one of the major ways to advance in a teaching career. Ralph Duffy, another veteran of the teacher-shortage days, came 'up' to the secondary school from primary teaching, and has trained in bits and pieces, upgrading his qualifications as he went, some at university and some by correspondence. A number of teachers in the study were plodding through the long march of a part-time degree. Teaching, like other semi-professional occupations, has been getting more credentialised.

Every teacher has stories to tell of the first year of teaching. Let me quote one from a teacher not involved in this study, who crystallises the whole thing beautifully:

> The First Form classes are given to the least experienced. It's a stupid educational ploy—if you don't get them at once, you lose them... I'd get butterflies, diarrhoea, and the rest, before I met them each day. I arrived tense in these classes, so I was probably a goner before I began. I was never given any ideas about how they might be handled, about strategies. It was very difficult to keep up with the number of different things I was required to teach them; a quite unexpected hazard of the job. I wasn't very good in those days at inventing a technique which made them do all the work; I had to get on top of content for every class, and teaching Weather, the Ganges Plain, Volcanic Landforms, Tax Forms all in the one day overwhelmed me. A first year out teacher spends the entire time totally exhausted from reading and thinking and planning, never mind the bloody emotional trauma of it all.[12]

Those who survive this kind of experience understandably feel they have passed a very severe test. It is a source of pride and self-congratulation; one of the strongest forces bonding teachers emotionally to their job, feeding into a sense of solidarity with others who have been through the same initiation. Humorous horror stories about it are a recognised hazard of teachers' social occasions.

After the trauma of the first year or two comes the move off the bottom. The deputy in charge of the timetable eventually gives you better classes; you get more confident about control, pick up some tricks of the trade, perhaps move to a more agreeable school. You become a little settled in the job; as Mary Coleman put it (p. 151), 'This is my fourth year out, and finally I think I'm starting to become a reasonable teacher'.

At this point a nebulous but important decision is likely to be made, perhaps best formulated as the choice between a career-structured approach to teaching and a non-career approach. Those who are moving onto the career track start to accumulate Brownie points: further qualifications; time spent doing extra jobs around the school such as supervising clubs; administrative-cum-counselling work such as being form mistress or house master; overseas experience. They may try to develop a specialty, becoming the school's audio-visual expert, computer expert, slow-learners expert. In the state system they will apply to be put on promotions lists; in the private system they may move from school to school to widen their experience and contacts. The eventual goal is a headship, or more remotely a senior job in the administration. Directors-General are always ex-teachers.

Those who do not take this approach may simply not see themselves as spending a lifetime in the teaching trade. Andy Gallea and Mary Coleman, though enthusiastic teachers, both look forward vaguely to something else in a few years' time. Teaching is also something you can leave and return to. Several of the older women we interviewed had done that, after breaks (up to seventeen years) caused by child care and husbands' careers. Both the exit to alternatives, and the re-entry, are more difficult now in the recession.

All that is reasonably familiar. What is less familiar, and perhaps more interesting, is teachers who have rejected the career path though they do have a commitment to teaching as a lifetime enterprise. Joe Guaraldi, whose abrasive encounter over probation has been noted (p. 129), speaks with considerable distaste of the way you have to crawl to authority in order to get promoted. Terry Petersen (chapter 3), though experienced enough to get another step, has rejected further promotion as it would destroy his work as a teacher. Administrative promotions (to deputy) take you out of the classroom, while curriculum promotions mean you lose your base in a particular school. Jack Ryan (chapter 5), another long-serving teacher, has more important work to do in his school and in the local community than he would be likely to find elsewhere.

Though there is an element of survivorship about both Terry and Jack, increasing length of service has also meant increasing personal investment in being a teacher. This is an important case, as there are at present incentives for experienced teachers not only to move out of the classroom, but also to move on from a given school. If state schools are to become organic to working-class suburbs, it is necessary for teachers to be able to find both personal and professional satisfaction in sticking with them. The issue of 'permanency' as it has been taken up by teacher unions in Victoria is a crucial one.

One always thinks of careers as going up; they also go out. We only interviewed practising teachers, but several had left in the past, or wanted to. Jeremy Hansen 'got really fed up with teaching', Len Johnson got tired of the 'drudgery', Rosa Marshall got totally frustrated in the state school. Several others were contemplating getting out when we interviewed them, including Doris Willoughby, who is feeling terribly tired, and Faye Taylor, who does not like ordering people about. And a couple of teachers nearing retirement look back with mixed feelings: Margaret Atwill, who basically likes it but has found it more and more of a strain, and Ralph Duffy, who sums it all up:

> I've enjoyed some of the time teaching, other times I sort of wish I'd never taken it on. (laughing) But I suppose that's common.

Divisions among teachers

The idea of a 'career' or path in life stresses what teachers have in common. It is equally important to consider the profound divisions among teachers caused by the organisation of schooling and its intersection with larger social structures.

There are, in the first place, divisions that follow from the internal arrangements of the teaching trade. The teachers we interviewed were in secondary schools, and most of them had never taught outside a secondary school. A small number had experiences such as teaching in primary schools before coming up to secondary, doing a little university tutoring, or some part-time further education classes. But for the most part the division between levels of the education system is sharp.

Within the secondary schools, the division that often strikes teachers most forcibly is that between subject departments, especially where the division of subject-matters also involves differences of method and equipment, and educational ideology. This is very much less visible to the pupils and their parents, who hardly ever refer to it in discussing schools. Among the teachers it can be a source not just of division but of conflict, even serious antagonism.

Length of service is important in teaching, in a number of ways: as a source of personal commitment to the occupation, as a source of informal authority in the school, as a measure of skill in the trade, and as seniority in the public-service sense, a means of access to promotion and positions of power. Here the larger social structure of age relations in our society, which concentrates power among the middle-aged and old (but not the very old), takes a definite form among teachers. Youngsters like Andy Gallea and Joe Guaraldi feel their exclusion keenly. Another young teacher, Sheila Goffman, is in a much stronger position largely because she is supported and protected by an older person, her head of department.

These patterns provide a kind of institutional grid within which teachers locate themselves. The division of subject departments, however, is something more, it is also bound up with the politics of the curriculum. The hegemony of the competitive academic curriculum drives a wedge between the teachers who are mainly involved in the business of academic achievement, and the teachers who are mainly responsible for one or other of the subordinated curricula. On a range of educational issues these two groups are likely to have divergent perceptions and opposed interests.

The curriculum is also implicated in the most vexed issue of general educational outlook, the division between 'progressive' teachers and their opponents. As already mentioned, the staff at Rockwell High are divided into two camps along these lines. There are disputes over assessment, integrated sport, streaming. The subject departments tend to line up, with English and science on the progressive side, manual arts and mathematics on the conservative. As this alignment suggests, the progressive/conservative division is by no means a case of non-academic departments *vs* academic ones. But the competitive academic curriculum and the instructional and selection practices connected with it pose some of the central issues on which progressives and conservatives dispute: teacher-centred pedagogy, streaming, university-based curricula, and formal examining not least.

The other great issue on which a progressive/conservative division opens up is 'discipline'. The staff of Greenway High are currently split on this one, as Len Johnson reports:

You get interpretations of rules. I look at the spirit of what is

being done, and I don't really care if the kids—in what way
they're doing it, and I tend to bend all the time, just so long as I
can see the kids are genuine and not just mucking around. And
there are other teachers who really think that any time anything is
transgressed it must be [hammered], and if everybody did that then
we'd have perfect discipline. There's such a diversity of opinion on
discipline.

The Greenway staff have been wrestling with it at staff meetings
and 'rules days', without making much progress.

Teachers are also divided by the two great structures of social
relations, gender and class. The structure of gender relations
makes a primary division between women and men, and we have
seen plenty of evidence of how this division works among
teachers. There is a division of labour in the form of subject
specialisation, and another one created by the survival of sex-
segregated schools. Men as holders of authority—certainly of
most of the promotion positions—commonly supervise women;
women in turn find it hard to gain authority and are faced with
extra difficulties and complexities in exercising it. Men as holders
of power tend to defend men's privileges; some women teachers
(and some men too, though fewer) contest this, challenge sexist
attitudes, argue for equal opportunity programmes.

Gender relations among the kids throw up problems of control
as well as curriculum, to which teachers respond in divided ways.
Some tackle questions of sexuality head-on as important
pedagogical issues, others avoid them like the plague. At a more
subtle level, the gender system divides teachers not just as
between women and men but also in terms of different ways of
being women or men: Doris Willoughby as a 'battle-axe', Sheila
Goffman as a good mate, Margaret Blackall as a 'strict big
sister'; Alan Watson as Babbitt, Andy Gallea as the male lead
from *Hair*, Len Johnson as Lucky Jim... This in turn feeds
back into practice as teachers construct personal versions of
progressivism, conservatism, and some teaching styles not
recognisable as either.

The main way the class structure divides teachers is the
separation of the elite private schools from the public school
system. The basis of this separation is the class situation of the
schools' clienteles, though there is also some class difference in
the recruitment of teachers.

The schools in our study do not constitute a sample of the

state and private systems in general; they include only a specific kind of state school, and do not include the majority of 'private' schools, the Catholic systemic schools. But the sample does have a broader coverage of the Independent sector; and as many of the teachers have moved around, their experience covers a wider spectrum than the schools in our study. We have at least strongly suggestive findings about the public/private division.

Perhaps the most striking point is that it is hardly an issue at all for the state school teachers. Many of them are almost unaware of the existence of the private schools. They did not go to them, they never visit them, they have no sense of them impinging on their own work. The public school teachers who do know a bit about them, usually older teachers, take a mild and tolerant attitude. Margaret Atwill, for example, assumes their existence is due to peculiarities of the parents, such as religious enthusiasm, and therefore they do not concern her.

But the public/private distinction is a big issue to *private* school teachers; even, I would venture to say, The biggest issue in their educational world. This is so whether they approve or disapprove of private schooling. Some private schoo teachers are either ambivalent about, or opposed to, private schooling. One thinks the conformism of the staff 'positively unhealthy'; another that you simply should not be able to *buy* education; a third that the private schools are bastions of class privilege. Working as teachers in schools they disapprove of is more than a little contradictory; the issue is inescapable for them.

The majority of the private school teachers, however, approve of private schools. They recite the familiar litany of parental choice, better discipline, educational quality, the need for diversity. Private schools are said to offer more stability of staff, more personal contact, more knowledge of the kids. James Christianson, a headmaster and an experienced publicist, insists he is not *against* the state system. The private schools are simply *different*; let us have diversity, who could be against it in a democratic society?

The trouble is, as noted in chapter 9 (p. 00), the private schools must pit themselves against the public system. And they do. The image of the public system held by private school teachers who support private schooling is unrelievedly negative. Rigid bureaucracy, heavy-handed supervision, slack teachers, uncontrollable kids, drugs, sex, religious and moral indifference, homosexuals, are all rolled out. Even the size of state high schools is exaggerated, for example, the estimate of 'two and a half thousand' quoted on p. 113; the actual average for New South Wales high schools is 830, and for South Australia near 600. Our research was not designed as an evaluation study, but it did yield a lot of information about teacher–pupil interaction. It gave no grounds for thinking that such familiar claims about the private schools as having more dedicated teachers, staff in general knowing more about the kids, or higher standards of teaching, are generally true.

One might wonder, looking back over this catalogue of divisions, whether it makes any sense to talk of 'teachers' as a single group at all. Certainly the somewhat glib definitions of the 'teacher role' in old-fashioned sociology of education textbooks look at bit sick when set beside this reality. Yet there are some forces that push towards at least partial unifications of teachers, among them teachers' own ideology. That is the subject of the next chapter.

Summary, chapter 10

Teaching can become central to the kind of person you are. Particular kinds of femininity and masculinity are reflected in teaching, and often set up conflicts about authority, careers and families. Masculinity and femininity are themselves changing, with many teachers caught up in the changes. Patterns of entry to teaching—via family, other teachers, or later-life choice— reflect social and historical relationships. Formal training is thought less important than the drama of the First Year Out. Some teachers enter a career pattern while some work out a commitment to teaching that does not involve climbing ladders. Teachers are divided among themselves by the institutional arrangements of the education system and the school, by their responses to educational issues, and by the impact of the social structures of gender and class. The public/private division is important particularly to private school teachers.

11

Teachers' outlooks

Concepts and knowledge

Our research asked teachers to talk about particular kids as well as their job in general. As they did, we gradually became familiar with a system of categories that most, though not quite all, deployed. It is possible to sort out four main types of categories used in describing the kids.

The first is a set of terms that have to do with their *success at formal learning*: academically 'good' or 'strong', 'weak' or 'poor', 'average', 'middling', and so forth. It was the bottom end of this spectrum that was most in focus, and attracted the most varied and colourful language: 'dodoes', 'dum dums', 'thick', 'low standard', 'plodder'. Terms for the other end, like 'university material', were pale by comparison.

There were two significant variations on this theme. Some teachers used the name of a stream ('an F or G student') or a track ('commercials' *vs* 'generals') to characterise the students personally. More widespread was the use of concepts that made academic success the effect of some embedded quality of the person: 'able', 'low IQ' 'bright', 'dull', 'capable', 'high potential'. In a number of cases it is quite clear that this ability is assumed to be a fixed attribute of the person, not affected by teaching, nor by effort at learning. A teacher who thinks this way may talk of a boy performing 'above his ability', or parents as well as kids having to come to terms with limited ability.

The second set of concepts is implicitly contrasted with ability; it has to do with the *energy or enthusiasm* a pupil puts into formal learning. One is 'a trier', another is 'slack'; one is a 'hard worker', another 'will not work' at all. 'Stubborn', 'lots of drive', 'persistent', 'conscientious' are other variations on the theme of motivation. Mary Coleman neatly rings the changes on the two axes, speaking of working-class kids who are not being selected by the school:

> I think you can divide them into two categories: those that can work and won't, and those that can't work and won't.

The third set of concepts has to do with the *disruptiveness* or otherwise of the kids' behaviour. 'Quiet' *vs* 'noisy'; 'cheeky', 'behaviour problem', 'trouble maker', 'hell in the classroom'; and the balm of 'normal easy-going kids'. The phrase 'good student' was often used in a way that implied 'easy to get on with' as well as, even instead of, academically successful. As the theme of academic success was implicitly theorised into ability, this theme could be implicitly theorised by appeal to a tacit understanding of the normal pace of development. A disruptive kid can then be classified as emotionally immature, and one who gives no trouble as mature.

The fourth set of concepts is less clearly defined than these; it does not define a familiar axis for the classification of kids so much as the kind of idea teachers reach for when the others will not serve. Trying to explain something puzzling that went wrong in their relationship with a pupil, teachers will speak of a 'personality clash'. What is being suggested here is a notion of individual *temperament*. Different kids are described as 'disorganised'; a 'manly little bloke'; a 'mouse emerging'; and so on. Obviously such notions can merge into those of disruptiveness and of motivation, but there is also something more complex being suggested here, a notion of the way the whole personality is organised. With some teachers this broke the bounds of all summarising adjectives and became complex and vivid accounts of individual personalities. Some teachers are first-rate empirical psychologists.

Teachers also have categories for describing where the kids come from. Much the most heavily trafficked are the notions of 'good homes' and 'bad homes'. Good homes are educationally supportive and emotionally stable. The parents take an interest in the kids' schooling; there are two of them; they are at home in the evenings, and while there, don't just booze and watch TV. Bad homes commonly have broken marriages: 'Quite frankly', says Doris Willoughby, 'most of the kids that we have trouble with here, we find there's a divorce or a de facto.' Or they have husbands who get drunk and thump their wives, or have no steady job. The parents leave the kids to their own devices, take no interest in the school, spend all their free time in the pub or the club, and do not have books in the home. They are slack, no-hopers, and probably their kids will be the same.

We heard so many variations on these themes that we came to regard them as a kind of organic sociology produced by teachers. Also reasonably common was the idea of a class difference between teachers and pupils in the state schools. Teachers are 'middle class', as Terry Petersen asserts (p. 28), while the kids are 'working class'. Sometimes the bad home is assimilated to the notion of the working class as a general explanation of the school's troubles in controlling the kids and getting them to learn. This yields an image of the school as a kind of middle class life-boat adrift in a sea of proletarian roughness. Other teachers make finer class distinctions and locate the bad homes in the lower depths of the working class; this gives them an explanation of why some kids do knuckle down to school work while others rabble round and drop out. Some who have come in contact with academic sociology of education gloss all this with the notion that working-class kids cannot appreciate the school's offerings because they are culturally deprived.

A minority of teachers resist such ideas. Jack Ryan has been discussed in some detail (chapter 5). Ralph Duffy is one of the few teachers at Greenway High to live in the school's catchment area and, while as an old hand he accepts many of the standard categories used in the teaching trade, he will not apply notions of cultural deficit to his neighbours in any simple form. Some teachers—Joe Guaraldi (p. 104) is one—even begin to formulate a sociological argument about the way the school as an institution produces reactions among the kids; this however remains rare.

The private school teachers often have the same sociology of families, with the twist that their ideological conflict with public schooling invites them to allocate the bad homes to the state schools and the good homes to their own. The parents of the latter have, after all, proved that they do care by forking out to pay the school fees. Beyond this, there may be very little under-standing of the school's social milieu at all. We came across teachers with quite naive ideas about who they were teaching; believing for instance that an elite private school contained a cross-section of society. There were even a couple who repeated the very silly (and offensive) argument that the families who send kids to private schools are the 'disadvantaged' ones, because they pay fees as well as taxes to support schools.

On the other hand there are teachers in the private schools, especially older teachers, who have an exact, extensive, and sophisticated understanding of their clientele and its economic position. One of the most impressive pieces of empirical sociology I have ever come across was James Christianson's off-the-cuff analysis of the changing social geography of the district his school draws from, the corporate structure and family connections of the city's financial establishment, the changing occupational background of the families who use the school, the impact of professionalism on the demand for education, and sundry other matters. No one else produced quite such a tour de force, but others like Angus Barr (chapter 3) certainly know their way around the family and business network connected with a particular school, and around the private school world at large. It is necessary knowledge for anyone interested in becoming a private school principal, who will be constantly concerned with fund-raising and the school's position in the market.

Classroom teachers are not called on to acquire that kind of information. Their professional knowledge is more focussed on their subjects' content and methods. The knowledge of how to teach is both intricate and elusive. Only the most elementary forms of it can be formulated in the language of the 'methods' units in teacher training—how to plan a lesson, how to use audio-visual aids. This is far from being knowledge of 'how to teach' as an accomplished skill. If teachers are agreed on anything about their trade, it is that you do not yet know how to teach when you have just finished the DipEd.

It follows from what has already been said (pp. 126–7) about the enormous complexity of the act of teaching (at least, teaching well) that it is extremely difficult for a teacher to describe her knowledge of how to teach, to express it in formulas. Much of it takes the form of intuitive decisions about what to do at a given moment in a given classroom, how to respond to a given student's difficulty in grasping a given point, and so on. Yet this *is* knowledge, and very important knowledge, which should be given a full measure of respect in the process of educational reform. Proposals that in effect press teachers to follow they can concentrate on how she or he is going in their subject. Andrew Sutting puts it with characteristic bluntness:

> As their maths teacher that doesn't concern me at all. I just roll in for that maths group. I really don't know what class they come from; except when I do assessments, and then it is just a matter of paperwork anyway. So that doesn't concern me.

There is an honourable reason for this blindness: teachers know about halo effects and prior judgments, and do not want to be prejudiced against any child who appears in their classes. As Mary Coleman says, 'I judge the kid on what he is, not what his parents are'. But there is also a willingness not to know about things that might be too hard to handle.

The major reason for teachers' lack of real knowledge of the families is simply lack of time and occasion. For most teachers a full working week—given the range of tasks listed in chapter 6—does not leave room for sociological exploration around the school's catchment. It is not provided for in the time-table, nor in teachers' industrial conditions. Nor are teachers generally trained or encouraged to do it. Many teachers say frankly that the only occasion they learn about pupils' families is when there has been trouble. Then they will go and check the record card for details of the family, or talk with a parent who has come up to the school. For the most part they must rely on what they hear from the kids, and what they hear from their fellow teachers. Staffroom conversation, ranging from virtual case-conferences to casual gossip, is an important influence on individual teachers' perceptions of kids and of the milieu. It is a major support of the common categories already discussed, and of broader educational and social ideas.

Images of teaching

An important element in teachers' thinking about teaching is the belief that it is a socially responsible, and hence dignified, job. Margaret Atwill insists (p. 98) that she is not about to be an 'entertainment' for students, just filling in their time; Arlette Anderson is scathing about being a 'glorified baby-sitter'. The notion that it is a responsible job is compatible with very different interpretations of who one is responsible to, but in any form it implies that teachers should give a full measure of commitment to what they are doing.

With Margaret Atwill it is clear that the dignity of teaching is very much bound up with the ability to teach your subject properly, that is, with the academic curriculum. Most teachers have been selected in the schools through the competitive academic curriculum; some came into teaching as a result of their parents' attachment to this form of culture. It is likely to be close to both their personal and professional identities. This is more than a matter of their 'values'. As teachers like Margaret Blackall (chapter 1) and Rosa Marshall (chapter 4) show, it is a matter of *practices* in the fullest sense, of the way whole lives have been conducted.

One way of conceiving teaching that is compatible with the academic curriculum is through its structure of credentials. Glen Moncrieff (p. 81) is one who is constructing a full-blown professional identity this way, moving through a string of postgraduate qualifications and carving out that hallmark of professionalism, a certified specialisation. He is annoyed with the lack of professionalism of other teachers who do not keep up with new developments in the field through their journals.

This is only one of a number of versions of professionalism. Another is Angus Barr's (chapter 3), where the notion has less to do with technical certification and more to do with respectability and social status. Perhaps a more attractive side of professionalism is shown by people like Alison Chant (pp. 80–1), Rosa Marshall (chapter 4) and Bettina Alt (p. 70). These teachers get a keen pleasure from the exercise and refinement of a highly-developed expertise. The key to their professionalism is the notion of professional autonomy, the ability to control their own work and the space to develop their own practices. Professionalism fuels their resistance to pressure for conformity from management and parents.

The notion of an independent responsibility is important in yet another version of professionalism, espoused by teachers like Joe Milwell. To him it has the sense of meeting tough challenges; teachers rely on their professionalism more, he suggests, as the difficulties of classroom control rise. The skill involved is practical and interpersonal as much as a question of certified knowledge. But the skill is not exercised in a moral vacuum; it is applied in the context of an ethical commitment to the interests of the kids. The teacher is responsible for one side of an exchange: doing the job thoroughly, knowing its circumstances, formulae are likely to be seen as an assault on their hard-won practical knowledge. They really do need space for creativity to do their job.

The inarticulateness of teachers' knowledge of their own trade is perhaps one reason for their willingness to accept bits of over-articulate knowledge that seem to offer a scientific base for their profession. Professions are supposed to have secret knowledge which lay folk do not have. Much the most successful candidate for this role in teaching is intelligence testing. Here is secret knowledge (the text of the tests being confidential, and the calculations and their statistical basis esoteric), and a scientific-sounding language for talking about the kids and explaining what teachers are greatly interested in—whether the kids do or do not learn. In some schools the IQ is regularly calculated and much store is set by it. Many teachers use the terms 'IQ' and 'intelligence' loosely, as a version of the concept of ability or academic success. None that we spoke to mentioned, or seemed to be aware of, the academic criticisms of the concept and the tests.[13] Yet some did seem uneasy with it, reaching for notions of temperament or motivation or hard work instead; and some used no general ability concepts at all. The science of intelligence has not become universal in teachers' thinking.

These categories of thought are closely related to the practice of teaching, to the organisation of the labour process and the social relations in schools. This is very clear for the two major axes of 'ability' and 'disruptiveness'. The ability concepts express the way the competitive academic curriculum sorts people, as individuals competing with each other in terms of their speed in moving through a hierarchically organised body of knowledge. Ability concepts offer a generalised explanation of success or failure in teaching, which shifts the responsibility away from the teachers onto the presumed nature of the child. This psycho-logisation of what is actually a social relationship is a very important mechanism of ideology. The ability concept likewise offers an individual explanation of the institutional process of pushing kids out of the education system. At a certain level So-and-so is said to have reached the 'limits' of her or his ability.

The disruptiveness concepts arise directly from the teachers' task of imposing order and maintaining discipline, and at a second remove from the state of hegemony in the school. Once again, there is a psychologisation: the social relation of discipline and resistance is projected into the kids as their personal attributes. There is said to be difficulty in imposing order because the kids are immature, or troublemakers, or whatever. Or there is none, because this is a nicer bunch of kids. Teachers who have left the state system for private schools often talk in this vein about their new pupils, how much 'more pleasant', 'civilised' they are.

In both cases the categories are produced by disconnecting the school's end of the social relationship involved, and folding the relationship up, so to speak, into the pupil's breast pocket. Something similar goes on in the construction of the 'good home/bad home' schema. Most often the teachers who use these notions do not know anything at first hand about the kids' actual homes. For instance Jeremy Hansen offered a favourable characterisation of one pupil's family; its basis turned out to be that the kid had never given trouble, and his textbooks were always neatly covered with brown paper with a waterproof plastic cover over that. It was obviously a good home. Mary Coleman talks of some bad ones at a previous school:

> The homes that are around Hopetown, a lot of them are really lower class rather than working class. And you heard some pretty horrifying tales from people about what the home life was for some of the kids, when we were there. And actually, the guy who lives next door to us—he's the sales manager of Betta Bred Bakery in the Hopetown area—and he's been into some of the homes there, and he said some of the things that he's seen he honestly just couldn't credit. He said he never would have believed that homes could be like that till he'd been there. I think it's the sort of home that these kids come from, where a lot of the parents don't seem to have any expectations for their kids. They're not interested in them getting on. Whereas a lot of the parents here are interested in seeing their kids get on in the world.

As a matter of cold fact she has never been in these homes. As far as concerns her, the school might be an ocean liner and the kids arrive each day on dolphins; it is as isolated as that.

This lack of information, with Mary as with some other teachers, is deliberate. They do not want to know the family background, class situation, ethnicity, or whatever, so they can approach each kid on her or his merits, 'as an individual'. They do not want to know about the rest of a kid's school life, so looking out for the real interests of the kids. There is no implication in this notion of 'professionalism' that being a teacher justifies any privilege or prestige whatever; Joe is hostile to pretentiousness of any kind.

That sentiment at least is shared by other teachers who do not think of teaching as a profession at all. Terry Petersen (chapter 2) insists it is a job, not a calling, with fixed limits of time and emotional involvement. That does not stop him from feeling a strong sense of solidarity with other teachers, and being a firm supporter of the teachers' union. At this end of the spectrum, the image of teaching is rather more like a skilled trade than a learned profession.

There is no way of resolving the divergence, because in some ways teaching is like each, and in other ways like neither. The implications of different views do conflict with each other, especially on questions of unionism and solidarity among teachers. Glen Moncrieff's credentialised professionalism leads him quickly to a belief in individual advancement and a lack of concern with teachers' collective interests; he was the only teacher I remember offering the view that teachers in general were overpaid. Angus Barr's status-oriented professionalism favours quiet unions, if any. Alison Chant's professionalism is compatible with strong unions, and may need them if the heat comes on from the authorities; Joe Milwell's is too. Terry Petersen's conception of teaching demands active unionism.

Perspectives on education

Such differences about the nature of teaching feed into divergent views of the larger purposes of education. These may be stated in a general way or—as will be described shortly—embedded in practice; in both cases there was a significant degree of conflict among the teachers we spoke to.

General views of education fell into four main groups. The first is focussed on intellectual growth. Education is above all a matter of enlightenment, of broadening the understanding. Margaret Blackall, insisting she is here to teach about ideas, not jobs; Glen Moncrieff, criticising the inbred school for lack of intellectual stimulation; Alex Stimson, who believes in a rounded intellect and has got himself a BA as well as a BSc because scientists are only 'half educated'; Mary Coleman, who wants the kids to think about big ideas, wrestle with concepts, above all, think for themselves; all are talking dialects of this language.

This view of education often pits the teacher against the demands of parents, and sometimes against the official line of the school too. Teachers can stand on this ground to fight the principal if need be. It gives teachers a cultural mission of some dignity. The resulting attitudes can be condescending, when mixed with notions of 'cultural deprivation' among the natives, but can also be supportive for kids grappling with the contradictions of their worlds.

The second approach stresses the notion of individual development and pictures the teacher as a kind of gardener encouraging the kids to grow and flower. This is the classic territory of 'progressivism', at least of its individualist wing; and Sheila Goffman is a classic example of what it means in practice. Len Johnson illustrates a more astringent and individual outlook which still lays its major emphasis firmly on the interests and personal development of the kids.

This approach can be inflected towards a concern with the politics of teacher-pupil relations, as with Joe Guaraldi and Andy Gallea, who value above all an open, honest dialogue. This informs their sharp criticisms of the existing education system. Or it can be inflected towards a psychological concern with individual personality, as with James Fenimore, who is trying to organise a weekly meeting of all teachers dealing with Year 9 in his school as a kind of case-conference, to work through each kid in turn, pool information, and plan treatment.

The third stresses the importance of the transfer of skills from one generation to the next; intellectual skills, of course, included. This may take the form of a concern for 'standards', in a broad sense. It may take the form of a more pragmatic concern about training for jobs; though this does not necessarily imply a narrow conception of skills. Andrew Sutting, who argues that schooling has to be about skills and jobs, is also quite clear that the school cannot be responsible for specialised job training, only for the provision of basic and general skills.

This may sound a constricted view of education, but it should not be underestimated. It places the emphasis squarely on the process of teaching, here conceived of as instruction. The sense of identity *as a teacher*, as someone who gets kids to learn, is very important to teachers. Knowing that the kids in their classrooms were simply not learning was important in the demoralisation Rosa Marshall, Arlette Anderson and others went through.

The fourth approach sees the school principally as the transmitter of customs and values from one generation to the next. This may involve some responsibility to purify social values, as in John Welton's vision of an age of violence being leavened by the school's injection of humane values and refined culture. More often, however, the customs and values are given and the school's business is to attach the kids to them.

Where the enlightenment model readily justifies conflict with the values of the home, this leads to an attempt to align the two institutions. Julius Abnernethy makes this clear in discussing why parents send their kids to private schools:

> I really think it is the desire of the parents to see their kids get the best possible education. And I'll extend that to even the good homes, where they want to see their principles reinforced in the school situation. And I think from that point of view, we serve a *very* important function, extremely important. I'm whole-heartedly behind it. Because there's nothing worse than having a double standard, where the home is good and then at school you get a teacher who's indifferent to these things. And conversely where you've got a teacher who's conscientious and the home is a bad one, it makes the kids confused.

'There's nothing worse than a double standard'; the principle leads to the kind of closed universe in private schools that Glen Moncrieff deplores. The contrast with the teachers who set themselves to give the kids 'the other side' of the story could hardly be greater. Another contrast is with teachers who emphasise the transfer of skills. Alex Stimson, who also teaches in a private school, refuses to concern himself with how the kids dress, whether they speak well, or such matters. He is there to teach people who want to do physics.

As this shows, there are some stark contradictions between different teachers' general views of education. In practice these are muted in various ways. One is that different ideologies tend to have different institutional bases. The fourth perspective just outlined seems to have a much stronger presence in the private schools than in the state schools; the third mentioned is more likely to be found in maths staffrooms, the second in English staffrooms, and so on. But the more important factor is that general ideas about education do not translate easily or evenly into practice. Teachers with strongly opposed ideas can often jog along with each other reasonably well in terms of the routines of the school. The demands of survival come first, so a teacher may have to become reconciled to doing much that she or he disapproves of.

Such contradictions between principles and practice are by no means rare; nor do they all go in the same direction. Margaret Atwill announces herself as 'a very conservative person', and states that she would be quite happy to see non-academic kids drop out as soon as possible; yet her practice as deputy is very much directed to resolving the conflicts and problems that might make them do this, and helping them to stay in the school. Margaret Blackall and Lorraine Smart express sympathy with the kids and opposition to streaming, but in practice are active upholders of the competitive academic curriculum because of their attachment to knowledge and enlightenment.

On top of this, many teachers do not try to formulate general principles of education at all. Phyllis Howell declares that her educational philosophy is 'fairly, probably primitive', and retreats from a discussion of the principles behind the school's policies, though she is a thoughtful and innovative teacher and quite happy to discuss streaming, curriculum and other questions as concrete issues. At the other end of the spectrum of experience, Roy Clive, the football hero, is sceptical of all theory, plainly feeling he doesn't need it; he taught for a couple of years before beginning his training, and treats teaching as a self-evident practice that needs no intellectualisation. Angus Barr's much more complex educational outlook is also internal to his practice, embedded in what he does rather than stated abstractly in advance.

In place of theories of education these teachers have what might be called operating principles about how to be a teacher: something between a rule of conduct and a style of approaching the world. These principles are often shared by teachers who also state general philosophies. They are perhaps the most interesting thing about teachers' ideologies.

One of the most notable is well expressed by Jeremy Hansen. He was, he said, formerly an active supporter of the teachers' union, but is utterly opposed to strikes. Like Angus Barr he thinks teachers' public image has gone down hill because of union militancy. Teachers in his view should be socially con-

servative: 'they should be agents of change but they shouldn't
direct it'. The example he gives is that teachers should dress
sedately. He then tells a story against a feminist teacher who
came to his school, refused to dress conventionally, and did not
last more than a few months. He sums it up:

> I think it would be dreadful if we were apathetic; but it's just as
> dreadful if we're radical. You've got to find a nice even course
> down the middle.

This notion of going 'down the middle', of mediating between
extremes, of not being fully committed so as to be able to hold
the balance, is very attractive to teachers. For one thing, it is
safe; the parents won't come breathing down your neck. For
another, it fits well with both the personal development and the
enlightenment perspectives on education, with the teacher as wise
guide through the perplexities, or bearer of uncontaminated
knowledge. With a number of teachers this becomes a way of
looking at the world in general. Margaret Atwill is one. Talking
about social change, she carefully balances off the benefits of
progress with the loosening of family ties and sexual morality.
Talking about politics, she presents herself as a person who
avoids the extremes of opinion, doesn't vote Labor but very
nearly has, and would rather like a centre party:

> I rather regret the two–party system. I know a number of parties is
> supposed not to be good because it breaks up the power and you
> haven't got any solid body that's got a policy that will get through;
> but I hate this 'we're right, you're wrong' all the time. That
> annoys me exceedingly.

That is very characteristic—even to the extent of Margaret
balancing her opinion in favour of balance, by citing the
counter-argument in favour of polarisation!

Another operating principle prescribes moderation in a more
positive sense, insisting on realism, reasonableness, and practicality as principles of opinion and conduct. Alan Watson
describes himself as 'reasonably moderate in most things', with
equal emphasis on adverb and adjective. Jack Ryan is almost a
militant realist.

This shades into an attitude of modesty about one's own
claims, opinions, achievements, and hopes. Ralph Duffy, after a
lifetime in teaching, makes no large claims. He thinks education
should encourage a thirst for knowledge and a desire to go on

learning, but acknowledges that schools are not very good at it. He also wants to register some achievements, however qualified, such as the fact that schools discriminate against blacks and migrants less than the outside world does. It is not hard for modesty and realism to go sour and become cynicism, which certainly is present among teachers. At its more attractive end, this attitude becomes a concern with practicality, with a search for what is workable, manageable, and (importantly) not harmful, in dealing with educational issues and ideas. The effective innovator is someone like Jack Ryan who shows that something other teachers have not done is in fact quite practical.

This in turn is close to another operating principle: reacting to issues in terms of survival needs as a teacher. No matter how attractive a proposal is in principle, if it makes it more difficult for you to manage a classroom, if it increases the emotional pressure on you, if it adds to the workload, then you do not do it. 'Practicality is the whole thing' remarks Len Johnson, who observes the principle in its breach. This is not as selfish as it sounds. Given the close interweaving of the practices of all the different teachers in a school, protecting one's own position is also protecting one's workmates. This reaction defines a kind of collective pragmatism, which is an important grass-roots base of teacher unionism.

Finally, a point which I do not understand very well but which seems important. There is a pervasive moralism about the way many teachers talk about their work. Not in the sense of grand debates about ethical issues, but in the way particular transactions and situations are read. The familiar formula of the 'bad home' as an explanation of kids' failure in school is above all a formula of blame. Kids who are difficult to control are very often seen as lacking 'responsibility'; the contrast with 'good' kids is a moral one. Note, for instance, the phrasing in Doris Willoughby's comments (emphases added):

> You are always going to have this minority in any section who are going to do *the wrong thing*, whatever it is; and whether it's throwing chalk or whether it's *misbehaving* in class or *misbehaving* in the yard, there is always the minority.

and in another teacher's outburst that the parents are 'lazy and insincere'. At one level this is an easy way out; you do not have to probe deeply into whys and wherefores if things go wrong because of bad people. At another level there is more going on here. This language obliquely expresses teachers' unease about being made responsible for things they cannot actually control. It certainly helps to drive a barrier between the teachers and the clientele of working-class schools. Many of the kids, and many of the parents too, sense a moral judgment and sense that it is not favourable.

Summary, chapter 11

Teachers' views of their work can be analysed in terms of the concepts they use, the knowledge they have, their pictures of teaching and views of education generally. The concepts used for discussing kids, such as ability and disruptiveness, good and bad homes, generally arise from the schools' own practices and psychologise the social relations involved. Knowledge of how to teach is intricate and intuitive, therefore difficult to explain or defend. Teaching is widely thought of as a profession, but what this means in detail can vary from concern with status to a radical concern with autonomy. General views of education variously stress intellectual enlightenment, individual development, skill transfer and cultural transmission. More interesting perhaps are the half-articulated operating principles that characterise teachers' work and opinions. Among these, striking a balance between extremes, emphasising reasonableness and realism, survival as a teacher, and a widespread moralism are important.

12

Teachers' politics and teachers' power

At the end of Part Two I noted how teachers can feel under siege from social change, and observed that they need to find ways of grappling with the social pressures that impinge on their work, rather than erecting barriers around the school. In this final chapter I will try to bring together the implications of our material for this problem. The first two sections consider, more generally than in previous chapters, the nature of teachers' involvement in the structures of class and gender relations and the politics they give rise to. The final section considers how teachers have been and are involved in the process of reforming schools, and what is needed to move this process in constructively democratic directions.

Teachers, feminism and gender relations

As noted in discussing the gender regimes of schools (p. 140), the politics of gender relations has become more active in recent years and has raised sharper questions for teachers, and about them. From the early 1970s women's liberation and gay liberation have questioned the schools' part in the communication of 'sex roles' and gender stereotypes. Contemporary feminism has had a significant impact on teachers, though by no means a uniform one.

Some of the women teachers we spoke to are themselves articulate and considered feminists. They have a clear picture of the social subordination of women, and strong feelings about it. They feel a sense of solidarity with the women's liberation movement, giving critical support, but support nonetheless. They use its language, talking of 'male chauvinism', 'sexism', 'women's rights', 'sisterhood', and the like. They include, among

younger women, teachers like Arlette Anderson and Rosa
Marshall; among older women, teachers like Alison Chant.

A larger number are aware of inequalities between men and
women, but do not align themselves with women's liberation or
call themselves feminists. Faye Taylor is one. She has a clear
understanding of the drawbacks of marriage for women, and the
way they are channelled into marriage by not being educated for
alternatives; she recognises misogyny among the boys she
teaches, and confronts them on the issue; she thinks that
women were treated as second-rate when she was growing up,
and deplores the continued marginalisation of women in
teaching. She sees herself therefore as part of the history of
women's fight for equality. But she does not see herself as part
of a movement, and consciously distances herself from 'women's
lib'.

There are also teachers who do not talk about issues of
equality in that way but who in a sense *live* a certain liberation
as women. Margaret Atwill is one such, the crucial move being
her commitment to a career back in the 1940s. Sheila Goffman is
another, an active, energetic and confident woman with articul-
ately liberal attitudes on sexuality, but nothing to say about
inequality.

The content of teacher feminism, including in that term both
the labelled and unlabelled versions, is worth attention. It is well
illustrated by Mary Coleman. She is sensitive to sexism on the
part of authorities, noting for instance that the principal of her
school doesn't like women and 'has as little to do with them as
he possibly can'. She notes the underrepresentation of women in
positions of power, such as the fact that there is only one
woman among the senior staff at her school, who has 'an awful
job being stuck in administration with all men'. She is sensitive
to, and angry about, sexism among the boys she teaches; noting
for instance of one ethnic group, 'they're treated like little gods,
they're brought up to think they're definitely superior to
women'. As important as any of that, she is a strong, undefer-
ential woman who stands up for her own ideas in a milieu
dominated by men. She does not have a theoretical language for
talking about sexism, she does not even use that word. And her
idea of what schools should do is satisfied if they treat boys and
girls with formal equality:

Now girls can do metalwork, boys can do cooking, all that sort of stuff, if they want to.

That is to say, Mary is in favour of 'equal opportunity' but not of 'affirmative action'. This is common among teachers, and stems both from their outlook as teachers—the desire to balance between extremes, to be practical—and from the way they perceive the issue of gender. For many can see *inequality*: unequal access, discrimination against women, and the like. But few perceive *relations of power*, that is, the subordination of women, and hence a need for action to eliminate men's power. Bettina Alt, characteristically, says she believes in the principle of 'men's lib' too. The bottom line is that women who can see inequality between the sexes can often see no case for special treatment for girls; that would be 'discrimination' too.

This kind of feminism is not necessarily a weak belief. With a number of teachers it is clear and, in its own way, militant; it fuels an active engagement in re-shaping schooling to make sure that girls get their chance to prove they can do as well as, or better than, boys. Yet it is circumscribed. One way of expressing this is Myra Elsborough's. She is adamant that girls should be guaranteed an equal chance for academic advancement, but women 'shouldn't try to be men'. Another way is by drawing back from women's liberation as a movement, characterising it as extreme or unreasonable in its demands or language; again, a reaction that fits in with common features of teachers' ideology. Most important, teachers' feminism focusses on the consequences of inequality rather than the causes. It is relatively easy to mobilise support among teachers for improving the provision of academic training for girls, and difficult to get support for attempts to break down sexism among boys—or men.

Feminism has had an impact on the men in the teaching trade, too, though by no means as strong as its impact among women. The commonest reaction, among the men who discussed the issue, was a cautious acknowledgement that there was indeed some truth in what the women were saying. (A strength of the pattern of 'teacher feminism' is that concentrating on unequal access makes it easy to document irrefutable cases about discrimination, and focussing on remedial action is practical in a system where most of the power is held by men.) This leads a number of the men we interviewed to support 'equal opportunity' policies and anti-discrimination legislation. Cautiously, some agree with changes in the sexual division of labour.

A fascinating insight into the contradictions and ambivalences involved is given by Glen Moncrieff, in a passage which I cannot forbear to quote at length:

> Women are totally equal. Except I guess in matters of physical strength. I was good friends with a couple of women truck drivers once. There was one who used to take off a load better than any man. When you'd stop for the night, she'd jump into the sleeper cab and she'd put her skirt on and blouse and change out of her jeans. I do a hell of a lot of women's work in the house. My wife does a hell of a a lot, all the sort of things that a man would normally do in a sort of chauvinistic setup. I don't mind changing the kids' nappies. I wash the nappies. Maybe because the buckets are too damned heavy for her to take downstairs. I quite often bath the kids, things like that. By the same token, she'll wash the car or paint the walls or things like that. I can't see any reason why women aren't just as equal, particularly in academic [things]. *What about women with children working outside the home?* I disapprove. When they're very young. I think that the most formative years are very important. There's no doubt. Jane will go back to work when our youngest is at school, in three and a half years' time, because we want to buy a home.

Of course Glen agrees with equality for women; he would hardly be a real professional if he did not. But each concession he makes in theory he immediately takes away in practice. Women are equal—except in physical strength. A woman makes a good truckie—but then she puts on skirt and blouse again, so she's a real woman underneath. Women are equal in academic ability—but *they* have to give up their careers to stay home and look after the babies. In other passages Glen says long hair for boys is OK, provided you can still tell the sexes apart; and though he used to be 'narrow-minded' about homosexuality, he discovered that some of his best friends were gay, and is now quite tolerant about it.

What is going on here, I would suggest, is part of the wider process of the modernisation of hegemonic masculinity through the adoption of a rhetoric of equality and tolerance while sustaining most of the sexual division of labour and definitions of gender. Though the limits of this change are obvious, it should not be dismissed either. It is attractive especially to younger university-trained men, and offers some purchase for counter-sexist programmes.

The next most common reaction to feminism among the men was scorn and disregard. Jeremy Hansen sounds off against 'the women's libber who ruins it for females in general' and tells a hostile story about the feminist teacher who would not dress properly to suit his conservative boys' school. Angus Barr's remarks on married women teachers ruining girls' schools have been quoted (p. 45–6). (The people he thus dismisses include Alison Chant, Bettina Alt and Myra Elsborough.) James Christianson is patriarchal in the ruling-class style that assumes women simply do not count in big matters, and can be dealt with by jocular patronage at other times. There are other versions, but this is perhaps enough to indicate the style. The men who show it include some of the most powerful people we interviewed. Together with the other characteristic reaction of men in authority to issues of sexual politics, which cannot be quoted because it consists of not seeing that there is any problem, this makes for a powerful opposition to change.

Finally, we came across some traces of those contradictory and almost comic figures, feminist men. With some teachers it was just the faintest touch, such as John Welton's belief that this is the age of the male in decline and women coming into their own (p. 157); apart from his wistful remarks about how much nicer it would be to teach girls, this has no discernible effect on his practice. Clive Brimcombe, however, does teach in a girls' school, and is trying to divest himself of patriarchal authority (p. 156). The trouble he gets into is partly due to poor foot work, but is also a measure of the genuine difficulty of conducting a progressive sexual politics for heterosexual men.

Our study throws little light on the situation of gay teachers of either sex. Though there were doubtless homosexual people in our sample, as in any sizeable group, none had come out or were involved with gay liberation. The issue of homosexual people's right to work as teachers had been publicly debated in the years before our fieldwork. But it is easy to see why teachers would be cautious about asserting the point. The prejudice that homosexuals are some kind of threat to children dies hard. Yet the currents of thought just discussed also suggest bases for accept-ance, in the deeper concern with questions of gender, the awareness of oppression, and what we may hope is a reduced willingness to evade reality.

The varying reactions to feminism reinforce the importance of taking a historical view of gender relations. We cannot understand teachers by assuming an unchanging structure of patriarchy, for instance. The sexual division of labour, the subordination of women, and the oppression of homosexuals are all achieved in a social process that is dynamic and often turbulent. Teachers are not related to this dynamic externally, they are *inside* it, they live it.

Doris Willoughby, for instance, grew up in a family where her father would not let her mother take a job, at the cost of poverty for the family. Her mother's frustration fuelled a determination to see that Doris got the chance to become a teacher. Doris's own marriage has been constituted very differently from theirs, as among other things she earns more than her husband does. Her history shows not only the distance travelled in a generation but also something of the dialectic by which change is produced. Faye Taylor also notes the historical change, and indicates some of its irony:

My grandmother was the controlling factor in her household. She decided everything that would be done, and I think this was because she was the more intelligent of the two. Her husband worked very hard but she directed him. Which meant that she was in control. My mother from the time she married was, I suppose, controlled in that her finances were limited by what her husband gave her. But she had complete independence in what she wanted to do, how she wanted to use her time, what she could do within that. So that she always did what she wanted to, remembering that her responsibilities came first. So I wouldn't say that she was ever a second class citizen. But from my own generation, we could do whatever we wanted to do, remembering that when we left school and got a job, there were certain jobs that were not open to girls. The ones which were open to girls were very limited in pay and promotion, simply because it was expected that when girls married they would stop work. That has opened up. But with opening it up, there's been more of a definition of roles. Instead of being individual in your own right, you are now pushed into a stereotype *inferior* model, instead of being a *different* model. And in fighting for equality, some of the so-called double standards have been accepted where they never really existed before.

The historical change in gender relations has now reached the kids as well, remaking their relations with teachers. The most visible part of this is the hotting up of sexual politics among the kids and the changes in sexual mores that teachers like Margaret Atwill try to grasp with the term 'permissiveness'. Some teachers are not exactly delighted. Rosa Marshall, no prude, was horrified by the way the kids in a working-class school saw sex as an 'animal function' (p. 51). Jack Ryan, tolerant of many things, likewise finds the kids' sexual behaviour incomprehensible. But other teachers are up with the hunt. Alex Stimson was passing a pupil in the yard of the girls' school where he teaches just as she swore 'Jesus fucking Christ'; he replied drily, 'I don't think that's physically possible'.

The change is in practices as well as attitudes and language. Margaret Atwill reports increasing sexual harassment of the girls at bus stops after school. On their side, the girls have both become more sexual beings, and have asserted more control of their sexuality, in relation to boys and adults.

As Rosa Marshall's story indicates, the schools have made well-intentioned attempts to deal with these changes through sex education courses, discussions on ethics, and the like. Opinion among the teachers we talked to was that such courses were pretty useless, and sometimes a kind of comic catastrophe. The classroom context was wrong, the form was academic, or whatever. The conventional techniques of teaching, that is to say, give no grip on this aspect of gender relations.

At another level, however, teachers' responses have connected more firmly. The most developed examples are the renovations in some of the girls' private schools which have re-oriented them, through the academic curriculum, to the production of a femininity oriented to professions and an egalitarian model of marriage. In a less dramatic way, something of the sort has happened in the academic streams of working-class schools. No comparable change has occurred in the institutional definition and production of masculinity. There is at most a debate about masculinising practices, such as the cult of football, among teachers dealing with boys; with a body of opinion that it is much overdone, and some schools abandoning competitive sport. Hardly any of the schools we studied had formally moved into the territory of 'counter-sexist education' in the sense of Yates' useful article on recent theory and practice.[14]

Feminism has had a significant impact on teachers' outlooks;

conversely, teachers have become an important vehicle for feminism. The reasons for this are complicated, but certainly include the fact that teachers are intellectual workers, and that modern feminism developed mainly among intellectuals. The creation of secondary teaching as a mass occupation gave large numbers of women a new prestige and economic power. With the development of the coeducational comprehensive as the major form of mass secondary schooling, the 'amalgamation of lists', and other episodes of the desegregation of the teaching workforce, the occupation itself was a focus of tension in gender relations. And the fact that secondary teachers are, after all, dealing with adolescents all day, can hardly help but make them conscious of changing sexual mores and gender identities.

Teachers' feminism is, nevertheless, of a particular kind. To a significant extent it is the feminism of married women. Many are wives-and-mothers as well as employed teachers, and fall over backwards, as Phyllis Howell puts it, to prove they can do the job as well as anyone else. The reasonably good relations many of them sustain with their husbands no doubt inform their thinking about issues such as coeducation, as well as their preparation of girls for entry to professions on the optimistic view that there will be fair competition with men.

The impact teachers have on gender relations among the kids has a lot to do with the milieu they are working in. In the ruling class, patriarchal family structure and men's control of companies, elite professions, and major accumulations of wealth have meant in the past a very marked economic dependence of women. Here the schools have to some extent been creating a ruling-class feminism, through the offer of advantage in the race for professional access in the next generation. The point is well put by Phyllis Howell: many of the girls at St Margaret's have no particular career in mind, but think of themselves as being professional persons. The school supplies the academic tools. Even highly patriarchal families have bought this programme in order to protect their daughters' interests in what they understand are changed circumstances.

In the working class, economic dependence on men is less pervasive and a significant number of women are their own heads of households, are the major earners in a family, or at least make quite an important contribution to its economics. The ideological impact of conventional morality is weaker. As Terry

Petersen notes, many working-class people are living private lives that seem 'unconventional', by which he means *de facto* relationships and women running their own households. A kind of feminism already exists here.

But working-class feminism is very different from the feminism of the intellectuals. It is often manifested in schools as 'uncontrollable' behaviour by girls, sexual aggressiveness, hostility to the authority of teachers; things that define a pupil as a troublemaker not an ally. In this milieu, teacher feminism has almost totally failed to connect with the feminism of the teachers' clients. Its impact, rather, has been to split off one group of working-class girls from the majority through the mechanism of the academic curriculum, attempting to attach them to the teachers' model of career-oriented femininity. This is not an easy thing to do, and the tensions resulting, for the girls caught in the middle, can be severe.[15]

It seems reasonable to conclude that teachers are a significant force in the contemporary politics of gender; more so than the thinness of counter-sexist programs in the schools would suggest. They are far from being a unified force, in this realm as in others. Nevertheless teachers have become an important vehicle for some kinds of feminism among women and its supporters among men; and in certain contexts this is being transformed into a working educational program. This will remain a marginal achievement until the disjunction with the sexual politics of working-class neighbourhoods is overcome.

Class inequality

While teachers' place in sexual politics is still largely untheorised, it is different with their place in class politics. Here there is a firmly-established tendency among theorists to interpret teachers by analysing their 'location' in the larger structure of class relations (which usually makes them out to be members of a 'new middle class'), and to see them as agents of social reproduction, particularly as agents of the ideological subordination of the working class.[16]

As most of this book goes to show, understanding class relations is essential in understanding teachers. But I do not think an analysis which centres on the trigonometrical exercise of calculating a 'location' on an *a priori* set of theoretical axes, and reading off the political consequences, is the right way to do it. The collapse of this exercise into conceptual absurdities such as 'contradictory class locations' (in all seriousness, a *location* cannot *contradict*) is one clear sign that there is something seriously wrong with the procedure.

Rather than asking what teachers' class location is, we should be asking what class relations teachers enter. Better still, we should ask through what practices, their own and others', teachers participate in class relations; what their views, purposes and conflicts are; and what are the consequences for the making and remaking of class structure.

Teachers participate in class relations most obviously through their relationship with their employers. In the elite private schools the employer is, legally speaking, a small corporate entity; ideologically speaking, the school's clientele; and practically speaking, the head. The principal hires, though usually with the advice of a head of department, and determines salaries. Paul O'Neill, who has been teaching for fifteen years in such a school, observes that teachers' individual salary increases have been decided each year on the 'whim of the headmaster'; to get their increments, staff might have to threaten resignation. The head's position is strengthened by the secrecy surrounding the whole exercise:

> There has been the feeling of the school that money shouldn't be talked about anyway. We're gentlemen, we don't talk about these things.

Promotions are also in the principal's gift, and are used as a tool of policy. As with salaries, this is constrained by the market—a good teacher frustrated in one school may go to another—but a skilful principal will try to counter this by well-judged internal promotions or the promise of them. The head is also in a strong position to remove unwanted teachers. Usually some informal pressure will produce a quiet resignation, but sackings may occur. Both are more likely in the context of a school renovation.

Somewhat glamorised, as it is by private school enthusiasts like Phyllis Howell, teachers' conformity to the purposes of the school authorities appears as 'dedication', as a strong integration of the teacher with the school. Phyllis mentions, as signs of this, low absenteeism, taking on extra duties, and filling in for each other's classes. Others repeatedly mention longer hours worked by private school teachers. From a cool industrial-relations point of view, these are also signs of an insecure workforce; and one notes also how much unpaid labour the school is extracting. This includes more than the unpaid overtime, which is large enough. Male teachers' wives are also liable to be brought in, to work in the canteen, organise socials, stand in for the head's secretary, or help with the school play.

It is not surprising that there is some sense of a need to unionise, as well as a great deal of difficulty in doing it, given both the practical problems (a large number of small employers in an industry always makes organising a union difficult) and the ideological resistance. The result for a long time was very weak unions and no militancy. The balance of forces changed in the 1970s. In the later part of this decade private school teachers' associations were performing the impressive feat, for a union, of growing in strength during a recession. This was happening in several of the schools we studied, and we heard classic organising tales—secret meetings to avoid surveillance by a hostile principal, fear of victimisation, and so on. Much of the fire was directed against the arbitrariness in teachers' employment. The unions have pressed for a regular salary scale to replace the principal's 'whims', and generally to have terms and conditions of employment spelt out publicly. In the light of the common idea that professionalism and unionism are opposed to each other as forms of consciousness and organisation, it is notable that this move has been partly fuelled by the sense of professionalism which even teachers like Angus Barr, no friend of unions, approve. It is part of the dignity due to a professional to have clear-cut rights and security of employment, and not to be subject to arbitrary control, pressure, or dismissal.

For all this, a significant number of private school teachers regard the private schools as good employers, better than the state Departments of Education. What they have in mind, usually, is the dimension of control—bureaucratic structure, rigid curricula, arbitrary transfers—and a notion that the private school gives teachers more space to exercise their professionalism. I find this reiterated belief a little hard to accept. Not all private school teachers actually have that space. The image of the public system is rather anachronistic. The state teachers we interviewed, though they talked freely about their problems, rarely complained of oppressive bureaucracy. Further, the

patterns of control within the school (via principals and department heads) are quite similar for the two groups; while state
school teachers have a much more secure industrial position and
stronger union support in case of conflict with the employer.

Public school teachers' unions are strongly and long established, models of white-collar unionism, and their industrial
position at least is very straightforward. They tap into the
pragmatism and consciousness of shared experience already
discussed; they have, that is to say, cultural roots among
teachers as well as strictly economic ones.

As with any large unions there are differences of opinion
about their policies. While Joe Milwell thinks his union 'wishy-
washy' and Mary Coleman is irritated because 'all they ever do is
talk', Margaret Atwill is 'embarrassed' by the same union's
claims and does not support going on strike. But she does
support being in the union, which she thinks is essential for the
work it does for teachers. And that seems to be the guts of it: a
feeling that the union is an essential part of the teachers' world.
It is more positive than the embarrassed sense of a necessary
evil which seems to attach to private school teacher unionism.
Among public school teachers there is a real sense that the union
speaks with the teacher's voice and expresses the practical
realities and problems of teachers' lives in a way no one else
does.

If state school teachers are organised as workers in relation to
their employer, their relationship to their clientele, to the kids
and their families, is very different. Some state schools service
affluent suburbs, or professional and business families living in
socially mixed areas, but the majority service the working class.
In relation to this clientele, the teachers are the bearers of state
power. The state both provides schooling and compels attendance at it. This is, historically, the source of the 'discipline'
problem.

There is no doubt that, on the large scale, the way mass
schooling works serves to disadvantage working-class youth and
divide the working class. On the one hand the teachers of a
working-class school, in the situations they actually face, cannot
construct the practices which would sustain the high-powered
preparation for academic selection that occurs in elite selective
and private schools. Working-class kids in general are thus
objectively disadvantaged on entry to the labour market or in

selection for higher education. On the other hand, participation in this competition through the hegemonic curriculum selects out a part of the working class for advancement, and pits its interests against those of the majority.

Little of this is intended by teachers; least of all by those who hold an 'enlightenment' model of education which means they want to speak to the majority. But teachers' collective attachment to the academic curriculum attaches them also to the pattern of schooling which is actively producing the resistance and exclusion that sabotages such pedagogic aims. Teachers like Arlette Anderson and Margaret Blackall feel this contradiction acutely as a set of dilemmas in their own lives. Arlette and Margaret also show the main way teachers at present resolve the dilemmas, by developing a teaching strategy of control for the many and educational mobility for the few. Thus social disadvantage, exclusion and division are produced as mass effects by a powerful combination of teachers' survival needs in the face of the 'discipline' problem, and professional attachment to the academic curriculum. Put another way, if teachers in general are to develop educational practices that do *not* have these effects, that instead tend to unite and advantage working-class people, then other solutions to these two central problems must be available to them.

Some teachers, including Arlette Anderson and Terry Petersen, call themselves 'middle class' and half-ironically discuss teachers as missionaries to the working-class masses. Yet Sheila Goffman is right in insisting that 'some of us do' come from a working-class background and are strongly influenced by it—among the number, Arlette Anderson and Terry Petersen. It is not in any simple way true that teachers are middle-class bearers of middle-class values which they foist on the workers' kids on behalf of the system. Some teachers sustain a real identification with their working-class clientele, though often with qualifications or criticisms. Teachers have often suffered the 'hidden injuries' of class in their relationships with their own families: Margaret Blackall and Theo Georges for example, neither of whom is at all complacent about class issues. Teachers who are committed professionally to the academic curriculum, and the patterns of class hegemony it tends to sustain, are not passive agents of the system. They often try to take over the project, to do it on their own terms: as witness Joe Guaraldi and the biology curriculum,

Sheila Goffman and English, Joe Milwell in relation to discipline
(the pot smokers on the oval).

At the same time teachers do collectively sustain some derogatory beliefs about their clientele—the 'bad homes' stereotype
and the 'low IQ' concept are the most notable—that make it
easier for them to acquiesce in the negative things that are
happening as a result of their work. The elements of realism,
reasonableness, pragmatism, and refusing extremes that are so
important in teachers' outlooks certainly sustain teacher unionism and thus a clear perception of their standing as employees.
But they also give little encouragement to pursue issues beyond
what is practicable in the very short term. Often teachers understand very well what is going on around them, but within narrow
limits. Their social analysis is not so much wrong as incomplete.
The more horrendous bits of teacher ideology such as 'bad
homes' correspond to the areas of most ignorance.

Teachers in private schools are also involved in a more complex set of class relations with their clientele than might appear
on the surface. Some, though fewer than in the state system,
come from working-class backgrounds. Most of the clients of
ruling-class schools are richer, some very much richer, and many
of them better educated, than the teachers. In terms of the
ideology of private schooling the teachers are their employees.
This point is not easily forgotten. It was vehemently made by the
students at the school mentioned earlier (p. 112) who locked the
doors of the classrooms against late teachers and claimed the return
of ten minutes' worth of fees.

This understandably produces a degree of class resentment
among some of the teachers. It comes through in sardonic
comments about kids arriving at school in Jaguars, wandering
home across the polo field, and so on; and more formally in
widespread unease about the 'elitism' of the schools they teach
in. It is important in holding many teachers back from a full
identification with the private school system and the educational
interests of their employers. Insistence on their professionalism,
in the sense of a claim to autonomy and technical expertise more
than social status, is another important form of resistance.

Other teachers do make the identification, and there are also
good reasons for this. Some had a private school education
themselves, and many of them send their own children to private

schools, the schools encouraging this with reduced fees for their own staff. They may live in social networks which are at least on the fringe of the ruling class: Alan Watson's friends are mostly from private schools, and he first met his wife at a Rotary function. The sense of difference from the working class can be strong: Jeremy Hansen's house is in an affluent enclave in a mainly working-class region of the city, which he calls 'a little oasis in a sea of seething humanity'. (A paradigm for the private schools?) As Angus Barr illustrates (chapter 3), some private school teachers become not only integrated into the social networks of their clienteles, but active constructors of them. As we argued in *Making the Difference* the principal of an elite private school is without question a significant figure in the local ruling class, a specialist in its ideological problems.

In these ways teachers are involved in the corporate practice that constitutes the ruling class, attempts to produce some unity in it, and attempts to adapt it to changing circumstances. Yet this involvement has its dangers for the schools: too great a conformism, on the one hand; too much involvement in academic competition on the other. The competitive academic curriculum, however poorly it serves most of the working class, does not simply correspond to ruling-class interests. Many kids fail in the competition it sets up. Those who succeed may become more concerned with the form than the content, chasing extra marks, learning short cuts and exam technique, but failing to become full possessors of the dominant culture.

The practices through which teachers participate in class relations clearly do not constitute a single 'location' or produce a single set of effects. They are often at odds with each other and can be pushed in more than one direction. What is there in teachers' consciousness of class that might lead to a resolution in progressive rather than conservative directions?

Among many of the teachers we talked to, in private schools as well as public, there was a clear consciousness of economic inequality and social injustice. Margaret Blackall, for instance, comments very sharply on the concentration of wealth and power in Australian society. The staffroom at Auburn College was generally hostile to Malcolm Fraser's neo-conservatism, and consciously opposed to the parents' political consensus. The teachers there make sure the kids get a progressive line on

Aboriginal land rights. Ralph Duffy is sensitive to racial and ethnic discrimination; Alison Chant is skeptical of her school's brand of high-fee Christianity; and so on.

An aspect of the teachers' operating principle of moderation and reasonableness is a dislike of snobbery and pretension. This attitude is very widespread, from Jack Ryan pinching the Boss's personal parking space, to Terry Petersen's wariness of appearing 'a snob' in commenting on local families, Rosa Marshall's sneers at the la-de-dah manners her school inculcates, and Alan Watson's insistence that it is OK by him if a private-school pupil wants to be a motor mechanic rather than a doctor.

There is, we may say, a widespread egalitarian sentiment among teachers, and a good deal of information about the facts of inequality. There is, at the same time, much resistance to seeing this in class terms. The unwillingness of many teachers to bring the class situation of their pupils into focus—'I judge the kid on what he is, not what his parents are'—is important here. So, I guess, are their own interests as relatively privileged members of the workforce. The result is, in many cases, a political perspective that might best be described as progressive liberalism, and whose heroes are modernising right-wing Labor leaders like Whitlam and Dunstan. Margaret Atwill's desire for a centre party she could vote for comes to mind. A number of features of teachers' situation and outlook make progressive liberalism seem an attractive proposition, indeed common-sensical. Among them are their desire to mediate between extremes, and their unavoidable involvement in class politics but distance from the tougher aspects of the labour market and industrial conflict.

Two things can give a sharper edge to this egalitarianism. One is the impact of socialist ideas. Among the teachers we spoke to were some who knew the language of socialism, or even had some experience in the labour movement or radical politics. Rosa Marshall is one, as noted in chapter 4. The other force is teachers' own experience of being at the bottom of the heap, the identification some sustain with working-class life. Andy Gallea grew up in a dockside suburb, and has not forgotten it. He insists that kids from harsher environments are not inferior in nature, and when he talks about 'bad homes' he means material facts such as kids getting stabbed with a pair of scissors, or not getting enough to eat. Theo Georges grew up in the same suburb, and it shapes his approach to the kids he is now teaching.

> But in some things I'd like to help out, because I know, because I came from a poor background. We lived at the Dock area and we didn't have much. And we still don't have much, my parents still don't. And I like to see that everybody gets a chance, an equal opportunity, that I had. And if it's through schooling or getting a good reference or whatever, then let them have it.
> *Some people don't have a good chance?*
> Oh, I'm sure they don't. Yes, some kids have just been written off. 'He's a dumb bastard—look at him! Jumps around with yahoos!'

Theo's anger with the complacency and conservatism of his school's administration (pp. 133, 137) becomes clearer in this context. It is notable that this kind of experience rarely coincides with exposure to socialist theory. There are, in effect, two kinds of radicalism about class among teachers, which have failed to come together—or which have, historically, been prised apart.

Opposed to these trends is a range of conservatism. The staffroom at Auburn College may be anti-Fraser, but the staffroom at St Margaret's prefers not to discuss politics—or religion, or sex—at all. Jeremy Hansen, who likes to find a 'nice even course down the middle', is vehemently opposed to any notion of egalitarianism in schooling, believing that people are naturally unequal. Teachers' belief in 'ability' differences, sustained by the competitive academic curriculum and the programme of testing, can be turned into a belief in natural hierarchy in the world outside, with the streamed school as a prototype of the streamed society. One does not have to be a conservative ideologue to believe this; it can simply be taken for granted that inequality is justified by natural differences, things just work that way.

On the other hand some teachers are actively engaged in the production of conservative ideology. The principals of ruling-class schools, especially, have a platform and are expected to use it. Part of their job is articulating a defence of their schools and their clients' educational practices. This is not necessarily easy for them. One whom we interviewed was the child of a state school principal and had grown up in an atmosphere of teacher radicalism; understandably there was some personal tension involved in heading a christian institution devoted to the children of the rich.

But the job gets done, with a tool-kit of concepts about cultural difference, pluralism, the reconciliation of democracy and excellence, service to the community, emulation, discipline at school and purpose in the nation, and so on. The traditional speech-day version is a rhetoric pretty well disconnected from any specific reality but providing vague moral justifications for authority and inequality at large. The technocratic version lays more stress on competition, academic excellence, scientific progress and keeping up with the rest of the world. This is not 'reproducing' class relations unconsciously; it is very actively sustaining and modernising them.

Teachers in the process of educational reform

In neither class relations nor gender relations do teachers act as a cohesive social force. They are themselves deeply divided by the two structures, both in terms of their situations and their responses. Anyone who depends on a well-formed common response from teachers for an educational programme, whether conservative or progressive, will be sadly disappointed. But that does not mean teachers are either powerless as a group or immobile. On the contrary, their collective practice has clearly played an active role in the recent history of both class and gender relations. Movements of support for major changes in educational relationships have emerged among teachers from time to time.

One of the most important directions of change since the creation of the urban comprehensive high schools has been the move to decentralise control of them. This has had several strands: school-based curricula; institutions of 'community control' such as school councils; democratisation of the schools as workplaces, reducing the authority of principals; greater administrative and financial independence for regions or individual schools. Partly these changes have come through central initiative. They are good up-to-date administrative practice, and they have the happy effect of shifting some of the responsibility for the schools' problems downwards, too. Partly they have resulted from the pressure of teachers seeking ways of unblocking the gigantic log-jam in working-class education that had built up within the established organisation of schooling.

Yet teachers' responses have been mixed. For one thing such

changes create more work. Democratisation of the school means more time in committees; school-based curriculum means more time in research and preparation; options and flexibility for the kids mean more counselling, more timetabling shifts, more confusion to be sorted out. Without significant reduction of classroom contact hours or significant increase of support staff—neither of which has arrived—it is difficult for teachers to make these changes work. In some schools when we were interviewing there were already ironic complaints about 'too much democracy'. Where this was combined with a sense that the democratisation was a bit of a sham, that the principal still made all the key decisions, teachers' enthusiasm for these reforms could sink very low indeed.

Teachers' interest in relaxation of control and democratisation of the workplace is partly a professional one. It is a way of gaining the space they need to do their job well. The gains here have been real; the changing function of the Inspectorate is one measure of that. At the same time teachers' professional identity is at risk, and sometimes under threat, in these changes. Giving parents a greater say in the control of schools calls into question the claim to professional autonomy, and perhaps more damagingly exposes the weaknesses of teachers' work in areas where they do not actually have full control or effective solutions (for example, on discipline). And curriculum changes not only create more work, they almost inevitably have been couched as criticisms of the academic curriculum. Given the importance of academic knowledge in teachers' collective self-image, a powerful motive for rejecting such criticisms exists. The depth of feeling is illustrated in hostile comments about 'child-minding', 'babysitting', and 'entertaining' the kids. Thus there are both industrial and cultural reasons for conservatism on curriculum and control issues among teachers.

Yet the problems do not go away. If anything the difficulties of the secondary schools have increased. Teachers are practical people, the schools will still be there tomorrow, and some way of making them work has to be found. Sticking to the competitive academic curriculum and the received organisation of schooling is a feasible strategy, though there may have to be a bit of bloodletting to reduce the pressure and make it work. Margaret Atwill, a firm supporter of the competitive academic curriculum who is very conscious of the increasing strain teachers and schools are under, speculates about a solution along this track:

> I sometimes wonder—probably not at present because jobs are
> difficult, but if you ignore that for the time being—we'd be better
> with a lower school leaving age. Where if they wanted to leave,
> they left, got the job, and worked. And if later on they saw that
> that wasn't what they wanted, and they wanted school, perhaps
> some arrangement whereby they could come back.

This would reduce the comprehensive character of the secondary
schools, give priority to the academic streams and formal
teaching, and dump increasing numbers of working-class kids
out of formal schooling into short vocational and work-
experience courses or into the labour market itself. Something
like that is the neo-conservative programme for state schooling
as it has crystallised in Australia, the UK, and North America in
recent years. One can see why it can gain a constituency among
teachers despite their resentment of the education funding cuts
that go with it.

I think that policy represents a disaster for public education.
State schools, so conceived, are little more than ill-functioning
imitations of the elite private schools. Education is re-connected
with the labour market on the weakest possible terms, and
nakedly in the interests of the employers rather than the workers.
What is good in academic knowledge, notably its capacity for
generalisation, reflection and critique, is taken away from those
students who need it most.

To see the flaws in the neo-conservative program is easy
enough. To come up with a workable alternative is more difficult, though some progress is now being made, for instance in
the 'Manifesto for a Democratic Curriculum' recently published
by Ashenden, Blackburn, Hannan and White in *The Australian
Teacher*. In the final section of this book I want to reflect on
teachers' part in the process. A crucial condition for a workable
progressive resolution of the deep problems of working-class
schooling is what might be called the industrialisation of curriculum issues.

The assumption here is straightforward: *teachers' interests*
have to be protected in the process of educational reform, and if
possible engaged in making the reforms work. The competing
ideologies surrounding education give the emphasis to
everybody's interests except teachers': the needs of the child,

'parental choice', the needs of industry, the workers, the interests of society. There is constant pressure on teachers to sacrifice their interests to those of the kids, variously interpreted. Progressives too fall into this trap, pressing reforms of streaming, curriculum, discipline and teaching practice on the grounds that they are good for the children, with little attention to what they will do to the teachers. It is largely because teacher unions do insist that teachers have a distinct interest in the business, and often seem to be the only people saying so, that they have credibility with a lot of teachers who otherwise have little sympathy with unionism.

It is vital, then, to recognise teachers' interests in decisions about education as legitimate and important interests. Not just at the level of salaries, promotion rules, conditions of service. Teachers, like other workers, have a legitimate interest in the *content* of their jobs. They have an interest in doing socially useful work, in having a satisfying work experience, in not being under destructive personal pressures, in having space to be creative and exercise their skills. They have a legitimate interest in the *control* of their workplaces, in not being subject to other people's control without their consent, not being pushed around, having the opportunity and resources to make decisions collectively for themselves.

For 'legitimate interests' one can also say 'rights'. What is implied here is not that we should all sign declarations of the Rights of the Teacher, but that reforms of schooling should occur in a way that makes these things actually happen on the ground. The rights of children and parents are likewise to be respected, but not in ways that abrade those of teachers. When existing practices pit them against each other—for instance on 'discipline' issues—and create a demand for each to be compromised, it is a sign that the practices need fundamental rethinking and reconstruction to make them realisable together. This can be done, at the whole-school level, though it needs effort, imagination and care.

Thus the concept of schooling which is organic to working-class life in a way comparable to the organic relationship between the ruling-class school and its clientele, needs to be formulated in a way that recognises teachers' need for independence as well as a closer practical relationship with working-class families and neighbourhoods.

Where ruling-class schools are functioning very well, as is the case with teachers like Rosa Marshall and Phyllis Howell, it is in large measure because there is a *reciprocity* between the needs of the teachers and the needs of the clientele. They do not have to agree on anything much; Rosa for one holds left-wing opinions that would horrify many of her pupils' parents. The point is that their interaction is organised in a way that satisfies the teachers' needs for space, professional recognition, satisfying and rewarding work, and the families' needs for skilful teaching, academic advancement, a protected environment for the girls, and so on.

That kind of professional reward is possible in working-class schools too. Indeed, as some teachers point out, *more* professional satisfaction can come from doing well at what is historically the more difficult task. A reciprocity of interests plainly sustains Sheila Goffman's work, and—flavoured very differently —Jack Ryan's. Constructing an organic working-class school as an institution means finding ways of making that kind of reciprocity happen in the lives of the majority of kids and the majority of teachers.

The notion of reciprocity implies some means of matching teachers and situations. In the private school it is done by the market and the principals, hiring and firing their own staff. That is not compatible with the defence of teachers' rights as workers. But it is very important that there should be ways for teachers to pick schools, and for schools to pick teachers (including their principals) within the public system. Central monopoly of decisions about staffing is a real brake on the construction of a more organic relationship with working-class communities. The moves to change it, for instance in technical schools in Victoria, have large implications.

Organic working-class schooling is more than an abstract possibility. A number of schools have moved in this direction as bureaucratic control of the public system has relaxed, and their accumulating experience is now a very important resource for Australian teachers. At the end of this book is an appendix listing recent publications about seven such schools in South Australia and Victoria. None is necessarily a model for what to do in another school's situation, but at least the experience represented here goes some way to showing the practicalities of more constructive relationships between teachers and working-class clienteles.

The notion of a democratic curriculum, which would give priority to the interests of the majority of kids rather than the academically oriented minority, also has to be formulated in the light of teachers' interests. Here it is not so much a question of conflict with the interests of the students so much as a contradiction within teaching itself. On the one hand is teachers' attachment to academic knowledge, which I will emphasise again is not an 'opinion' one can put on or put off, but a personal relationship embedded in the whole pattern of most teachers' working lives. That attachment will remain. Yet the academic organisation of knowledge, and the competitive form of its appropriation in schools, is also a central cause of the educational failure of mass working-class schooling, and hence of public school teachers' difficulty in getting personal and professional satisfaction in their work. The drift to 'relevant and meaningful' curricula abandoned academic knowledge; the drift to 'standards' and neo-conservatism abandons the search for professional satisfaction and the rewards of good teaching. The idea of a democratic curriculum drawing on academic knowledge but refusing to accept the conventional forms of its transmission has a chance of transcending this contradiction.

Good teachers in working-class schools all too often are like plumbers in a crumbling house, dashing round to plug a leak here, open a tap there, put in a new pipe somewhere else. Good programmes in working-class education often have the same character: good repair jobs, but quite out of proportion to the scale of the underlying problems. I have described renovations of schools; what is at issue now is the renovation of a system of schools. That needs political will, and a mobilisation of resources beyond what teachers themselves control. There are severe limits to what they can do in education by themselves. But given the political will, the process crucially needs teachers' creativity. The ideas that will make it work will mostly come out of the space the system gives teachers to develop their practice. These ideas will grow mainly as a development of the intuitive knowledge at the core of teaching.

The title of this chapter names 'teachers' power'. This was partly to register the idea that teachers as an occupational group have some weight in the world, control significant institutions, and have to be reckoned with in the balance of social forces, a point that has perhaps been sufficiently shown. It was also to

suggest power as potential, power to do things, possibilities as
teachers. This is not so obvious. The conventional rhetoric of
education, even while stressing teachers' rôle in shaping the
hearts and minds of the next generation, casts them basically as
society's agents and invites them to submit to a fate they have
not made. This is profoundly pessimistic. It is also self-
defeating, since in the final analysis the next generation must
make itself. What teachers can do, with their students, is create
new possibilities, build paths into regions that have never been
explored before. And that is very close to the heart of teaching.
It happens on a small scale every time a teacher teaches well. We
need to translate it to the large scale.

Summary, chapter 12

Teachers have been significantly influenced by feminism in
recent years. Concern about sexism and support for 'equal
opportunity' provision is widespread among women, though
there is limited support for 'affirmative action'. Men are
divided about the issue, some hostile and some cautiously
supportive, few active. Teachers are involved in their own
lives in the changes in gender relations. Their practice in
the schools has been uncertain, more effective in some
ruling-class milieux than in working-class schools.
Teachers participate in class relations as employees. The
employment relation in the private schools is different in a
number of ways from that in state schools where unionism
is stronger. They are also involved in quite complex class
relations with their clientele, which are worked out in
different ways by different groups of teachers. There is a
reasonably widespread social radicalism among teachers,
muted in practice and opposed by several conservatisms.
Teachers have had an ambivalent relation to the decentralisation of control in education and progressive reforms of
curriculum. It is important that reforms take full account of
teachers' interests as well as those of other groups.
Teachers have legitimate interests in the content of their
work and the control of their workplaces. To create a
reciprocity between these interests and those of the
working-class clientele is central to progressive reforms.
Teachers' creativity as teachers is vital in making reform
work.

Notes

1   Holt, 1978, p.9.
2   *The Republic*, III, 415.
3   Particularly in the British work of Bernstein, 1971, and subsequent work on class and the curriculum. An American synthesis is offered by Apple, 1979.
4   For documentation of this movement in Australian schools, see the sources on particular schools listed in the bibliography; and for more general statements, *Who Owns The Curriculum?*, 1980; Cohen and Maxwell (forthcoming); and the reports of the 1983 National Curriculum Conference in Adelaide (ACSA, 1983 and 1984).
5   For this line of thought I am indebted to Michaela Anderson's as yet unpublished PhD research on teacher unionism in New South Wales and Victoria.
6   Town's argument is in an excellent chapter on 'limiting factors' on innovation in Scottish education, buried in one of the *Educational Priority* reports (Morrison, 1974). It deserves to be better known.
7   i.e. under supervision by a juvenile court after some legal offence.
8   This has now become an active area of theorising as well as empirical research. The most impressive theoretical analysis is offered by Arnot, 1981 and 1982; for a stimulating collection of articles see Walker and Barton, 1983.
9   Grace, 1978, p.218.
10 The Married Women (Teachers and Lecturers) Act of 1932 accomplished this. Some special categories were exempted; on the other hand women thereafter had to resign upon marriage. The episode is discussed by Mitchell, 1975, pp.112-3.
11 Hegemonic masculinity is discussed in Connell, 1983, chapter 2; and more analytically in Carrigan, Connell and Lee, forthcoming, where further references will be found.
12 From an unpublished description by Peg Baker, reproduced with her permission.
13 The class-biased character of IQ tests has been plain since the brilliant critique by Davis, published *in 1948!* For a more recent and

scarifying analysis of the history of 'mental testing' see Kamin, 1974.

14   See Yates, 1983. We have discussed renovation of a girls' private school in 'Class and gender dynamics in a ruling-class school' (Connell et al., 1981).

15   See the case of Elaine Markham in our booklet *Ockers and Discomaniacs* (Kessler et al., 1982) pp.7-8.

16   For examples of the trigonometrical approach to the class analysis of teachers in Canada see Harp and Betcherman, 1980, and for Australia, Harris, 1982. 'Reproduction' analysis has become very widespread in radical educational sociology since the publication of Bowles and Gintis' *Schooling in Capitalist America*. Apple, 1979, makes the most systematic application to curriculum issues. I have developed critiques of both tendencies as approaches to social theory in *Which Way Is Up?*, chapter 7 (on class trigonometry) and 8 (on reproduction theory).

Bibliography

General

Apple, M.W. (1979) *Ideology and Curriculum* London: Routledge & Kegan Paul

Arnot, M. (1981) *Class, Gender and Education* UK: Open University Press

—— (1982) 'Male hegemony, social class and women's education' *Boston University Journal of Education* 164 (1), pp.64-89

Ashenden, D., Blackburn, J., Hannan, W. and White, D. (1984) 'Manifesto for a Democratic Curriculum' *Australian Teacher* no. 7, pp.13-20

Australian Curriculum Studies Association (1983) *Shaping the Curriculum, Vol. 1* Adelaide: ACSA

—— (1984) *Shaping the Curriculum, Vol. 2* Adelaide: ACSA

Barton, L. and Walker, S., ed. (1981) *Schools, Teachers and Teaching* Lewes: Falmer

Bernstein, B. (1971) *Class, Codes and Control* London: Routledge & Kegan Paul

Bowles, S. and Gintis, H. (1976) *Schooling in Capitalist America* NY: Basic Books

Carrigan, T., Connell, R.W. and Lee, J. (forthcoming) 'Hard and heavy phenomena: The sociology of masculinity 1900-1980' (available from the sociology discipline at Macquarie University, North Ryde 2113, Australia)

Cohen, D. and Maxwell, T., ed. (forthcoming) *Blocked at the Entrance: Context, descriptions and implications of curriculum changes*

Connell, R.W. (1983) *Which Way is Up? Essays on sex, class and culture* Sydney: George Allen & Unwin

Connell, R.W. & Irving, T.H. (1980) *Class Structure in Australian History* Melbourne: Cheshire

Cook, K. (1967) *Wake In Fright* Ringwood: Penguin

Davis, A. (1948) *Social-Class Influences upon Learning* Cambridge, Mass: Harvard University Press

Game, A. and Pringle, R. (1983) *Gender at Work* Sydney: George Allen & Unwin

Grace, G. (1978) *Teachers, Ideology and Control: A study in urban education* London: Routledge & Kegan Paul

Harp, J. and Betcherman, G. (1980) 'Contradictory class locations and class action: the case of school teachers' organizations in Ontario and Quebec' *Canadian Journal of Sociology* 5 (2), pp.145-162

Harris, K. (1982) *Teachers and Classes* London: Routledge & Kegan Paul

Hawkins, G. (1982) *Resistances to School* Sydney: Inner City Education Centre

Hilton, J. (1934) *Goodbye, Mr Chips* London: Hodder & Stoughton

Holt, M. (1978) *The Common Curriculum: Its structure and style in the comprehensive school* London: Routledge & Kegan Paul

Kamin, L.J. (1974) *The Science and Politics of I.Q.* Potomac: Lawrence Erlbaum

Middleton, M. (1982) *Marking Time* Sydney: Methuen

Mitchell, B. (1975) *Teachers, Education and Politics* St Lucia: University of Queensland Press

Morrison, C.R., ed. (1974) *Educational Priority, Vol. 5: E.P.A.—A Scottish Study* Edinburgh: HMSO

O'Donnell, C. (1984) *The Basis of the Bargain: Gender, Schooling and Jobs* Sydney: George Allen & Unwin

Sennett, R. and Cobb, J. (1972) *The Hidden Injuries of Class* NY: Vintage

Walker, S. and Barton, L., ed. (1983) *Gender, Class and Education* Lewes: Falmer

Who Owns the Curriculum? (1980) Melbourne: Victorian teacher unions and parent organisations

Woods, P. (1979) *The Divided School* London: Routledge and Kegan Paul

Yates, L. (1983) 'The theory and practice of counter-sexist education in schools' *Discourse* vol. 3 no. 2 pp.33-44

Other reports on this research

D.J. Ashenden and others, 'Class and secondary schooling', *Discourse* (Australia) vol. 1 no. 1, 1980, pp.1-19

R.W. Connell and others, 'Class and gender dynamics in a ruling-class school', *Interchange* (Canada), vol. 12 nos. 2-3, 1981, pp.102-117

G.W. Dowsett and others, 'Divisively to school: some evidence on class, sex and education in the 1940s and 1950s', *Australia 1939-1988, A Bicentennial History Bulletin*, no. 4, 1981, pp.32-60

S. Kessler and others, *Ockers and Disco-maniacs: a report on sex, gender and secondary schooling*, Sydney: Inner City Education Centre, 1982.

R.W. Connell and others, *Making the Difference: Schools, families and social division*, Sydney: George Allen and Unwin, 1982.

G.W. Dowsett et al., 'Effortless good order? How a study of private schools throws light on the nature of discipline', *Radical Education Dossier* (Australia) no. 17, 1982, pp.9-12.

D.J. Ashenden and others, *The Democratic Curriculum* (Video and Kit), Adelaide: Focus Film Productions, 1983. (Part I of video based on this research.)

D.J. Ashenden and others, 'Making curriculum democratic', forthcoming in D. Cohen and T. Maxwell, ed., *Blocked at the Entrance*.

S. Kessler and others, 'Gender relations in secondary schooling', *Sociology of Education* (US), Jan 1985.

Sources on organic working-class schooling

An important theoretical and practical review of educational programs for working-class youth has just appeared: P. Dwyer, B. Wilson and R. Woock, *Confronting School and Work*, Sydney: George Allen & Unwin, 1984.

Recent experiences in particular schools which have developed effective relationships with working-class students and communities can be found in the following sources:

Sydney Road Community School, and other schools in the Brunswick area (Vic):

Gil Freeman, *Small School in a State of Change*, Melbourne: Deakin University Press and VSTA, 1982.

W.Hannan and G.Spinosa, *A Mediterranean View of Schooling*, Melbourne: Hodja/BRUSEC, 1981.

Bill Hannan, *The Democratic Curriculum: Essays on schooling and culture*, Sydney: George Allen & Unwin, 1985.

Kensington Community High School (Vic):

Les Cameron, Kerry O'Neill and Bruce Wilson, 'Class and curriculum —a basis for action', *Radical Education Dossier*, No.20, 1983, pp.4-8.

Mansfield Park Primary (SA):

Getting It All Together, Schools Commission film (available through their offices in all states).

David Pettit, *Opening Up Schools*, Ringwood, Penguin, 1980.

Parks Community Education Centre (SA):

Clare McCarty and Jac Rattley, *Acting Together*, Adelaide: Wattle Park Teachers Association, 1983 (available from W.P. Teachers Centre, 424 Kensington Rd., Wattle Park, SA 5066).

Sunshine High School (Vic):

David Jones, Michael Metcalfe, Trevor Williams and Jim Williamson, *The School Curriculum and Self-evaluation Project at Sunshine High School, 1976-82*, Task Force Report No.7, La Trobe University School of Education, 1982.

Elizabeth West Junior Primary School (SA):

Uri Bronfenbrenner, 'Our schools need a curriculum for caring',

Pivot, vol. 9 no. 2, 1982.

Michael Middleton and Pat Thomson, *Community Education and its Relation to Education Policy*, Deakin University, forthcoming.

Moreland High School (Vic):

David McRae, Rod Maher and Graeme Jane, 'Kids come here to "do". Moreland's school-work program', *Victorian Teacher*, October 1983.

Some very interesting New Zealand cases are discussed in:

P. Ramsay, D. Sneddon, J. Grenfell and I. Ford, 'Successful and unsuccessful schools: a study in southern Auckland', *Australian and New Zealand Journal of Sociology*, vol. 19 no. 2, 1983, pp. 272-304.

Index